"YOU'RE THE *DOCTOR* - YOU DECIDE"
-Growing up in the Blitz

Graham Matthews

Glenthorne Publications

2004

Published by
Glenthorne Publications
Glenthorne, Lower Camden, Chislehurst, Kent
e-mail: grahamf.matthews@btopenworld.com

ISBN 0-9547250-0-X

Printed and bound in the United Kingdom by
FOTODIRECT
Brighton, E.Sussex, 01273 563111

To my children and grandchildren,
for whom this little book is intended to provide a brief glimpse
of a fast receding history and possibly some amusement.

Acknowledgments

I wish to thank Carolyn Grace for permission to reproduce the photograph of Spitfire ML 407 and the National Archives for permission to reproduce the cartoon of the evacuee.

The efficient research on the ballet 'Le Festin d'Araignée' carried out by Patricia Collins at the Manchester Library and Information Service was most helpful in confirming the accuracy of my recollection.

My thanks also to David Powles who suggested that I record my experiences as an evacuee, to my wife Daphne for proof-reading, and to Alan Milnes, Brian Southam, John Naylor, Denis Bews, Peter Smith, Rob Bryant, Bee Matthews, Jill de Warrenne, Nicholas Matthews, Carol Mackay, Molly Fenton, Gregory White and many other friends who have given their assistance.

Chapter   1 . . . . .Sidcup 11

           2 . . . . .For the sake of art 23

           3 . . . . .Berlin 25

           4 . . . . .Holidays 29

           5 . . . . .Christmas 1938 33

           6 . . . . .Evil Thoughts 35

           7 . . . . . . .On becoming a pianist 39

           8 . . . . .Park House 41

           9 . . . . . . .The Day War Broke Out 45

          10 . . . ."The Few" 49

          11 .The Blitz 51

          12 . . . . .The 'Operation' 57

          13 . . . . .Bombed out! 59

          14 . . . . .DYB DYB DYB 63

          15 . . . . .Big School 65

          16 . . . . .Macky 71

          17 . . . . .Close Encounters 73

          18 . . . . .V1s and V2s 75

          19 . . . . .The Evacuee 81

          20 . . . . .Double Exposure 87

          21 . . . . .Eccles 91

          22 . . . . .Abersoch 95

          23 . . . . .Uncle David 97

          24 . . . . .Auntie May 101

          25 . . . . .Victory 103

          Bibliography 109
          Index 111

"You're the *doctor* - you decide"
-Growing up in the Blitz

Introduction

I have tried to recount my experiences in the light of growing up in the pre-war and wartime days by transporting myself back in time and recalling my thoughts and feelings as a child. It is into this light that I invite the reader to enter. In addition to the events which involved me during the war period, I have included, purely for entertainment, some of the minor disappointments in my young life which I determinedly brushed aside. It was also my intention to include a little of the history of a world war of stupendous enormity which took place in the lifetime of many people alive today.

Chapter 1

Sidcup

I would have had a sister named Shirley had she lived. When I was about seven years old my mother, Alice, told me about the death of my sister the day after she was born. The birth had taken place in a nursing home in Peckham. The midwife in attendance insisted that my mother needed all the rest she could get after her period of labour so the baby had to remain in the adjacent room.

I received the account of my parents' tragic experience of losing their one day old baby somewhat unemotionally. My mother recalled how she pleaded with the midwife as she was concerned about the baby and was firmly told: "Don't fuss, mother." Despite her anxious pleadings on hearing choking sounds coming from the next room, my mother's instincts to protect her child went unheeded.

In some ways the death of my sister was to be to my benefit. This seems a terrible thought but my arrival on the 22nd February 1932 at 41 Burnt Oak Lane, Sidcup, was met with much rejoicing. Judging by the drawerfuls of photographs I suspect that the Eastman Kodak Company's profits must have risen sharply during the 1930s. Aunts and grand-mothers queued to hold me and cooed appropriately as the Box Brownies clicked. My parents simply glowed with pride at their achievement following three long years from the loss of their first-born and were much relieved to have produced the handsomest baby boy ever.

My paternal grandmother Mary, who was never one to miss an opportunity to offer advice, commented that my mother would have difficulty in raising such a sickly-looking boy. To be fair to my grandmother she was not entirely wrong in her prediction as I was diagnosed to have asthma at the age of three which has plagued me on and off ever since. The asthma first showed up on a holiday in Cornwall and, without exception, severe attacks occurred every time we went away.

Grandma Mary

It is quite possible that I had a seminal influence on my parents' decision to move from Peckham to the Marlborough Park estate in Sidcup due to my mother's impending happy event (the word 'pregnancy' was not acceptable at that time and I cannot bring myself to say it even now). The new houses, costing in the region of £975 (a brick garage an extra £75), were all of the pebble-dashed semi-detached chalet style laid out in blocks with gardens arranged end-to-end.

My birthplace in Burnt Oak Lane (front bedroom)

Burnt Oak Lane ran along by the side of the Daily Telegraph Sports ground which, as soon as the war started, was systematically turned into allotments by the local residents to support the 'Dig For Victory' campaign. This event put paid to the cricket and to the occasional visit by a glazier to replace a broken pane in the French windows at the front of our house following a well struck 'six'. Below is reproduced the receipt dated 7th January 1942 (my father's 35th birthday) for the payment of ten shillings (50p) for a further year's rent of the allotment plot.

CHISLEHURST & SIDCUP URBAN DISTRICT COUNCIL

TREASURER'S DEPARTMENT, COUNCIL OFFICES, SIDCUP PLACE, SIDCUP.
Tel.: FOOTS CRAY 3081

No.

S. E. Matthews.

A.L.
10⁷
/055

ALLOTMENT RENT.

Please take notice that your allotment rent for the year ending 31st March, 1943. is as follows:—

	s.	d.
Year's rent to above date	10	–
Arrears of rent		
Total	10	–

This rent should be paid as soon as possible at:—
Sidcup Place, Sidcup, between 9.30 a.m. and 4.30 p.m. (Saturdays between 9.30 a.m. and 12 noon) or Public Library, Cedar Avenue, Sidcup, on Thursdays, between 10.30 a.m. and 4 p.m., or
Sent by post to the Collector, Council Offices, Sidcup Place, Sidcup.
Please send this Demand Note with remittance and it will be returned officially receipted.

J. GAFFNEY,
Treasurer.

RECEIVED the sum here stated in printed figures

PAID   Treasurer   £   s   d.

-7 JAN 42   159469   C0   10T055   PST— 4 ** **** 10–0

Living in Burnt Oak Lane and its environs in the pre-war years provided a very happy period for my parents and probably for many people following the General Strike in the twenties and the depression of the early thirties. I felt very secure in my small community. My parents played tennis at the Marlborough Park Tennis Club which had several *en tout cas* courts. On summer days at weekends I was often parked in my pram by the side of the court where my mother and father could keep an eye on me. It was there that I first became acquainted with my friend John Willes who was similarly parked alongside me in his pram while both lots of parents enjoyed a game of doubles.

From our house I could hear the chimes of the clock in the belfry of the Lamorbey Park Hotel where Captain Oates (of "I may be some time" Antarctic fame) lodged, so my mother informed me. The hotel was situated close to the Sidcup golf course which had large sand pits where we played on occasions after the golfers had finished with them. It was also a happy hunting ground during the war for souvenir collectors as, to my knowledge, at least one plane crashed there.

We lived in the Lamorbey area near Sidcup station situated on the Dartford Loop Line. We got to know the proprietors of many small shops almost as friends. Auntie Ivy who had a haberdashery shop, gave me a penny each day I marked off her calendar. I addressed any lady of my mother's generation 'aunt' but to the family I referred to them as 'pretend aunts.' She measured off lengths of material against a brass rule on the counter top and charged her customers at prices such as 'one and eleven-three' (one shilling, eleven pence and three farthings) a yard.

The milkman kept me happy by providing me with a milk bottle half full of water into which he had dropped a chunk of dry ice (solid carbon dioxide) so that I could trot up and down the pavement making chuff-chuffing noises like a locomotive.

In those days the milkman pushed his float on his rounds

The coalman's horse gave us an added bonus apart from bringing the coal, if it had left something useful for the roses. At an age when I could appreciate the value of material things, my mother would hand me a coal shovel and direct me with a nod and a giggle towards the prized heap to beat the neighbours to the draw.

Carter Paterson provided a very satisfactory service. All you had to do was to place in the front window their printed card which had the letters CP embossed on it and within a day a van would arrive to collect a parcel or the family holiday trunk for advanced delivery to its seaside destination.

Sidcup was made up of several distinct areas, one being the High Street, where one would find the usual banks such as Martin's with its golden grasshopper swinging over the entrance and grocers like Home & Colonial and the Maypole of fond memory. In addition to the usual run of retailers there was the occasional more exotic establishment such as Foxwell's saddlery which even by the thirties sold very little tack compared with their market in school satchels, suitcases, straps and football boots. There was a gorgeous leathery smell as you entered the shop.

One of the two picture houses Sidcup could boast was the High Street's Regal Cinema where I went with my father to see the 1943 Ealing Studios' film, 'San Demitrio London.' It was all about the surviving members of a crew re-boarding their severely damaged ship after having taken to a life-boat for several days. I was spellbound by the bravery of those sailors who risked their lives in the Atlantic convoys. Another film shown there was 'King's Row' in which I witnessed to my utter horror the decision to have Ronald Reagan's legs amputated when there was absolutely nothing wrong with them. I looked at my mother in disbelief that anyone could be so despicable. She said it was just a story.

My father was not a drinking man, far from it. The sherry was kept at the back of the bureau and only appeared at Christmas or when the church minister called. So it was all the more astonishing to me that my father, as he and I got off the bus in the High Street one day, went straight into the Black Horse (recently re-named 'The Blue Rose', if you please, although its former name remains on the brickwork). At that time it was not the most salubrious of public houses and certainly not the sort of place for a six-year-old boy. I tugged at the coat in front of me and asked what the wearer was doing here. The curt response from a rather gruff-looking man caused me to beat a hasty exit into the arms of my father who had been anxiously searching for me outside.

There was another case of mistaken identity when a little younger. As a treat (treats were always welcome whether unconditional or as a reward or bribe) I was taken to see 'Snow White and the Seven Dwarfs' on its first showing in London in 1937. For the most part I enjoyed the film but had to be consoled during the scary transmogrification scene when the wicked queen spelled herself into an old hag. On leaving the cinema I rushed out onto the pavement only to find that the skies had opened and people were hastily putting up umbrellas. I ran back into the foyer and dived under the skirt of a lady I was convinced was my mother, only she wasn't. In the darkness of the skirt's interior I hung on to her legs for shelter and security until extricated by my parents.

The stationery shop was owned by Miss Lane who had her private lending library comprising many thousands of books, mostly romances and whodunnits, which could be borrowed for one penny per day.

Mr Potter ran the bicycle shop where he would mend punctures for a few shillings and sold Dubbin used to soften and preserve leather football boots. He sold boxes of single caps along with a two-part metal bomb on a string and also coiled strips of caps in little cylindrical crimped cardboard containers for use in cowboy six-shooters. At risk of burning the top of your thumb you could set off caps by scraping a thumbnail along the strip. During the two weeks before Guy Fawkes' night, and at no other time, his front window was filled with an exciting array of fireworks. Rows of Brocks bangers and jumping crackers were stored under the glass top of his display cabinet against which I would press my nose. This versatile shop took in wireless accumulators for acid top-up and re-charge so that we were never deprived of the Home Service.

Many of the names of other shops in the area come easily to mind. There was George Higgins the hardware shop (still there to this day though much transformed) which sold screws singly and paraffin from the mysterious recesses at the back of the shop, provided that you had remembered to bring your own can. I arrived one Saturday morning on an errand for my father. The handful of nails I asked for were wrapped in newspaper and handed to me. I turned out the contents of my pockets in a search for some change in order to pay and placed on the counter a pocket knife, a conker on a string and various other treasures any normal boy would carry. I stuffed the things back into my pockets except for a rather grubby handkerchief which had glued itself to the counter top. He called me back with an "Oi!" and to my disgust added vulgarly: " 'Ere, yer left yer nose-rag be'ind!"

Mrs Dunn sold flowers (the shop facia still bears the legend 'Stanley Dunn' in copper-plate script); Eric Thomas fitted us out at the beginning of term with school uniforms; Butcher Curnow provided photographic equipment and developed films; Spicer's delivered the Daily Herald (no Sunday papers were permitted in our house); Chappell's undertook with dignity; and the South London Iron Company provided building materials. Opposite Holy Trinity church was the C of E primary school where I attended, the Post Office and the Odeon cinema. A large timber yard (now Travis Perkins) abutted the school playground and it was often necessary to climb onto the sawn trunks which had been stacked in spaced layers for seasoning, having at the ready the excuse of retrieving a ball should the foreman appear.

How Mr Goddard the grocer organised his window display was a source of continual puzzlement to me. I would hang behind outside the shop for a moment as my mother entered in order to work out how he managed to arrange in perfect symmetry lentils, rice, peas and other dried particulate comestibles against the inside of the window in large diamond patterns without the diamonds merging into one another. How was it possible to pile up grains of rice to form a flat inclined surface without the rice tumbling down. Without coming up with an answer I would hurry to catch up with my mother who had got to 'butter' on her grocery list and was handing over the ration books. More magic was being performed as the assistant would shape up, under my admiring gaze, an individual pound of butter with a pair of wooden pats having skilfully scooped from a huge block almost the exact quantity apart from the odd blob for make-weight. I liked the reciprocating motion of the guard-less manually-operated bacon-slicing machine although I was always anxious until the final cut of gammon had peeled off without injury to fingers. It took me a while to catch on when my mother whispered in my ear: "Have you heard the one about the grocer who sat on the bacon machine and got all behind with his orders." In those days we fell about at jokes like that. It could well have come from Tommy Handley's weekly radio show ITMA which bravely satirised Adolf Hitler and his cronies.

Roadknight's displayed in their window two very large bulbous glass jars containing respectively red and green liquid, the typical symbol of a chemist's shop. It was to here that I was to enquire furtively and naïvely for some sulphur, potassium nitrate (saltpetre) and carbon as I had recently discovered the formula for making gunpowder known, as I thought, only to a privileged few. With thumping heart and trying to look as casual as possible I asked for the first two components without any trouble but came unstuck on the powdered carbon. The chemist explained that she didn't have any but you could easily make some if you burnt some sugar. I abandoned the idea of making some by that method and instead resorted to collecting soot from the dining room chimney. I was quite gratified by my experiments and after getting the mix more or less right, produced a few modest bangs. I was able to improve my pyrotechnics as soon as I had dug out (with the use of a steel chisel!) some magnesium powder from an incendiary bomb I had acquired which resulted in bringing down a large area of plaster from my bedroom ceiling. The punishment for this went unfulfilled since, as luck would have it, for me at any rate, a few days after my otherwise successful experiment, the whole of the ceiling was brought down due to a nearby land-mine.

I have forgotten the name of the barber's shop next to the police station but not the ignominy of an incident which occurred there. No appointments in those days. You merely joined the end of the queue and moved around the room until it was your turn for the short back and sides which was the sole style on offer. I had arrived at a halfway position in the queue when the scissors stopped snipping. Without a word being spoken, the barber came round the circle of customers sniffing as he did so. I gulped when he stopped opposite me as clearly the signals he was receiving had indicated red alert. He demanded to let him see the soles of my shoes. Not for the first time in my life had I been trapped by a sensitive nose. I was immediately ordered out of the shop to remove the unpleasantness that I had trodden in.

In another cycle shop located a few doors along from the barber's it was possible to buy tins of calcium carbide. The stuff was sold for cyclists who still had lamps which worked with acetylene gas, not that I ever saw anyone with such means of illumination. Through the network I received training in yet another procedure for making very effective bangs. It was the age of bangs. A cocoa tin was adapted by making a hole in the bottom into which one end of a rubber tube was inserted with a force fit. The other end of the tube was sealingly connected to the screw cap of a bottle which contained calcium carbide. When water was added the mixture bubbled ominously. A hole was made in the lid of the tin through which the generated gas emerged. A volunteer was elected to light the gas and everyone retired to a safe position. Until the gas/air mix reaches critical explosive proportions nothing happens except for a little flame, thus adding to the suspense. The satisfactory bang is accompanied by the whole apparatus being blown apart. Harmless entertainment, we thought.

In Sidcup there were schools of every kind, several parks, recreational grounds, a golf course, a cottage hospital a few paces from the fish and chip shop in Birkbeck Road, a general hospital, a local police station with friendly bobbies and, during the war, a British Restaurant where for the price of one shilling it was possible to buy an ample three-course meal.

There were churches to suit all tastes. The church where I attended regularly with my father, who was the Sunday School Superintendant for twenty years, was the Congregational Church in Station Road (now a community church). The 3rd Sidcup Scout Troop and Wolf Cub Pack were based there. To be colour-bearer at the monthly church parades was indeed an honour and a very serious matter.

Sidcup Congregational Church
(Cubs, Scouts and church parades)

One often hears of Sidcup being used for the butt of jokes. However, as I have been reminded fairly recently by my friend David Powles, whom I first met up with at Eltham College in 1943, Sidcup provided for all our needs and was in reality a very pleasant place to live. The town where I was born and in which I lived for twenty-four years afforded a comfortable and happy life.

Chapter 2

For the sake of art

I do believe that my parents had a fetish in wanting to dress me up whenever they had the opportunity despite the fact that I was none too keen on the idea. I was told that I was very honoured to have been chosen to be page-boy at the wedding of a pretend aunt. The happy couple's entourage comprised four bridesmaids, a little page-girl and me. The little girl wore a long white dress with a wide green satin waistband, a big matching green bow and a white poke bonnet. She carried a posy of flowers which had trailing ribbons. A very nice outfit indeed - for a girl! To my undying shame I was kitted out in a frilly satin blouse, the sort that girls wear, satin trousers and white sandals. As a further insult I had to carry a posy and was instructed to hold the girl's hand.

The expression on my face gave no doubt as to how I felt.

Then there was the tableau fiasco at our church Sunday School. One Christmas, somebody had thought up the bright idea of putting on a show which included dressing up all the 'Beginners' to represent the children of the world in their national costumes. I was to be the little Dutch hero who put his finger in the dyke. Accordingly, I wore the statutory tall peaked hat and donned trousers onto which my mother had sewn coloured patches. The clogs I stood in were big enough to fit a large Dutchman of the kind I had seen in picture books, swallowing herrings whole. It was impossible to walk in the things so they were placed on the stage in a pre-arranged position and all I had to do was to step into them. We were all told not to move a muscle because this was a tableau. As the curtain was about to go up on the scene, the director noticed that I was clutching my middle and wriggling about. This was likely to cause a distraction, possibly some embarrassment, and might destroy the spiritual effect the tableau was supposed to engender in the audience. There was a minor hiatus as my mother was fetched to attend to me, whereafter I was whisked over the heads of the other children and hastily planted back into the clogs for the show to continue.

The children's Christmas party held in the January after the tableau affair was to include a fancy dress parade which afforded another opportunity for my parents to dress me up. This time I was Donald Duck. In addition to the duck mask with integral sailor's hat, I had strapped to my rear-end a box structure made of cardboard and balsawood representing Donald's distinctive tail. My legs were swathed in yellow bandages like puttees and my feet were encased in huge triangles made of yellow dusters sewn on to wire frames which in an earlier life had been coat-hangers.

As I stumbled in front of the judges I could barely see the participant in front of me because the holes in the mask did not coincide with my eyes. I was desperately hot and the wires of the webbed feet were sticking into my toes. I was glad when the proceedings came to an end. I left the hall clutching Third Prize.

Chapter 3
Berlin

My father, Stanley, qualified as a patent agent in 1928, the year my parents were married. At the age of twenty-one he was the youngest to have passed the patent law and technical examinations set by the Chartered Institute of Patent Agents. Incidentally, patent agents are now more appropriately renamed 'patent attorneys' and it was into this profession that I was eventually to enter with the patient guidance of my father. It is often wrongly supposed that we are Government officers. The Institute is an entirely independent body although it does maintain the list of Registered Patent Agents. Patent attorneys are hybrid creatures having knowledge of a scientific discipline and international patent law. They act on behalf of private inventors and companies in the Patent Office and before the Patents County Court where a smart grey gown is worn (but no wig).

The work my father was engaged in during the thirties included the licensing of patents. One of his clients, a Manchester firm (MEL), employed a group of brilliant scientists and chemical engineers researching into magnesium and aluminium alloys; light alloys as they are known. It was discovered that the tensile strength of light alloys could be improved by including small quantities of rare earth metals. MEL were prolific patentees who made their money by negotiating licences with companies manufacturing light alloys. One of these companies was I.G. Farbenindustrie who were producing light alloys for the German aircraft industry; correction, for the German *civil* aircraft industry we were given to understand (and, incidentally, for making V1s, see Chapter18).

Business necessitated that my father should make a number of visits to Germany before WW II. Years later he told me that he had stood in the crowd as Hitler passed by in a parade and was within six feet of him. When socialising with his German business associates in a beer kellar he was obliged to stand on the table while 'Deutschland über Alles' was sung, though he declined to give the Nazi salute. It was on one of these trips in October 1936 that I went with my parents to Berlin, my father having to settle another licence deal for the latest 'improvements in or relating to magnesium alloys'.

While I was in Berlin I was taken to the Brandenburg Gate where I saw the guards goose-stepping. I was also taken off to an exclusive photographic studio where I was unceremoniously seated beside a little German boy by the name of Hans Peter. I can remember making the most awful fuss. No amount of cajoling on the part of my parents or squeaking furry toys could console me. I don't think the fact that the boy's father designed bombs for a living had anything to do with it. I was just not in the mood for having my picture taken. The result (opposite) shows a remarkable feat of patience on the part of the photographer who managed to catch my surly expression as I took breath for another outburst.

My father's opposite number in Berlin was Erich Schubert , a thick-set eighteen stone gentleman with a lisp who was constantly clearing his throat. He would address my mother "Alith, my dear". It was he who promised that should war break out, his bomb-designer friend would design "...a nice little bomb to drop down the chimney of 41 Burnt Oak Lane." My father and Schubert were good friends so this dubious joke was treated with much hilarity, neither man being aware of the 'gathering storm' or more probably, not wishing to believe that there was trouble ahead. Schubert was captured by the Russians in 1945 and was not repatriated until 1950 when he was only seven and a half stone and thought to be dying. While he was away my parents sent food-parcels to his wife in Germany because she was experiencing severe deprivation. We on the other hand had received food-parcels during the period of the war from our American friends. I cannot cease to ponder the contradiction thrown up by our personal loyalties clashing with political interests.

Berlin 1936

When Mr Schubert came to England for my marriage in 1957, he hired the largest size morning suit that Moss Bros of Covent Garden had available; he was back to his pre-war weight.

Chapter 4

Holidays

Before the war Boscombe was my parents' favourite holiday resort. Here we hired a beach hut where my paternal grandparents would come and sit for a few days and dampen proceedings by complaining about more or less everything I did which gave me pleasure. They seemed to think that I did not enjoy dragging a pair of metal sand spades along the concrete promenade in front of them and scowled an order to desist.

My father did all the usual things for a small boy at the seaside. He would dig tunnels in the sand for me to crawl through. One day he built a turreted castle which resisted the remorseless tide until inevitably it became no more than a slight mound in the otherwise smooth newly-washed sand. For a treat I was allowed to stay up late to see the illuminations in the gardens along the front where there were displays of seals balancing rotating beach balls on their snouts and a sequence of lights depicting a batsman hitting a cricket ball and the ball's subsequent flight. The gardens had paths demarcated by candles supported in moulded glass pots suspended on metal stakes and chains of electric lamps hung between the trees so that the resulting strings of shiny pearls transformed the gardens into a fairyland.

There was also a boating pool in the gardens on which I sailed my clockwork speedboat made by Meccano (Registered Trade Mark). The clockwork ran down when the boat was in the middle of the pool and my mother volunteered to rescue it. She took off her shoes, stepped into the water and slipped on the slimy bottom of the boating pool and promptly sat down in two feet of green water. Thus ended what was otherwise a happy family day at the seaside.

In order for my parents to have an evening at the end-of-pier show unhindered by my attention-seeking, the hotel management had given

A3003

Broadstairs

assurances that I would be looked in on from time to time throughout the evening. I was duly tucked up, 'prayered', and left under the care of the lady of the hotel. An hour later one needed to use the facility which had been left under one's bed. I got up, locked the door to ensure privacy, performed as trained so to do, proudly slid the result under the bed and snugged back under the covers to fall fast asleep.

On returning some hours later, my parents found the bedroom door locked. Frantic knocking and calling were to no avail and accordingly extreme anxiety set in. With the help of the proprietor, ladders were fetched so that my father could gain access through the first floor window to find me sleeping peacefully. The cause of the trouble was soon discovered whereupon all of the windows in the bedroom were flung open for the purpose of very necessary and immediate ventilation. I was then woken up to be told how good I had been.

While on the subject of the seaside and at further risk of making all of my childhood memories related to bodily functions, I cannot forget my mother's consternation when my father entertained me by imitating a whale as he floated on his back in the sea. Spout after spout went up and the more I screeched encouragement with childish pleasure, the more he did it. My mother then noticed something bobbing about close to him whereupon *she* screeched: "Stop it, stop it." Blissfully unaware, he continued his whale act until my mother in desperation finally got the message home by shouting: "Stan——leeee, Richard the Third!" I had not cracked the code at that time.

Chapter 5

Christmas 1938

Christmas 1938 was a spectacularly White Christmas. It was extremely cold and the snow was many feet deep. What few cars there were crept slowly along the road making a muffled sound as the tyres crunched the snow, the headlight beams lighting up the gently falling snow-flakes. There was an altogether Christmassy atmosphere which was very exciting to a near seven-year-old. To add to the excitement, I was to have at any moment a brother or sister. At that time I was staying in New Eltham with Sydney and Margaret Slaughter and their children, Mary (5) and Judith (3). My father had become friends with Sydney as he too was a patent agent and had got to know him as they worked in the same London office for a time. The Slaughter family were to look after me once again, this time as a war-time evacuee, but more of that later.

My mother had gone into the Manor House nursing home in Sidcup (now used as council offices) for the birth of her third child. I awoke early in the morning of the 22nd. December as I had heard movement in the bed near to mine. I called out, mistakenly thinking it was my father who might have some news. A gentle voice belonging to an aunt of the family reassured me that my father would come to see me later that day and that I should get some sleep. Sure enough he arrived in the afternoon with the great news that I had a sister who was seasonally named Carol.

I stayed in New Eltham with the Slaughter family for ten days which was the period prescribed for hospital confinement at that time. Apart from a reprimand for encouraging the girls to say silly things to passers-by through the partially raised front room sash window from the safety of the now mud-coated settee, I received the full force of my host's disapproval a second time. The girls were having their nightly bath and I was temporarily in charge. Being in a tinkerish mood I filled a mug from the hot tap with what I thought to be acceptably warm water and for fun poured it over Mary's naked back. Her screams soon brought her mother quickly to the rescue and I was rapidly dismissed from duty.

On my return to Sidcup, there was my mother with the new baby and, so as not to downgrade my status, my mother sensibly involved me with all the skills of baby-rearing. First I was shown how to hold the baby in the crook of my arm so as not to let her head flop, a skill which I honed many years later with my children and grandchildren. I was intrigued with breast feeding especially when my mother inadvertently performed a good impression of Tintoretto's 'Origin of the Milky Way.' On asking her for an encore she swiftly told me not to be so rude. However, it wasn't long before this novel entertainment was denied me as my mother had to return to hospital for treatment for an abscess which resulted in the baby having to be bottle fed.

Cow & Gate was a cinch and I became skilled at preparing the bottle (a process which included first sampling several delicious spoonfuls of dried milk mixed with sugar), testing the temperature on the back of the hand, the deft insertion of the rubber teat (finest hole) between her tiny gums, and letting her chomp away without causing distress. After the ceremonial winding, as she stared, sated, over my shoulder, I was then able to carry out the nappy-changing routine which I can't say that I took to then or since for that matter with any degree of enthusiasm. Even at seven I was mystified by the physiological process in which a wholesome pure white liquid could be transformed by a sweet little baby into something partially solid and decidedly unpleasant.

Chapter 6

Evil thoughts

It was in Burnt Oak Lane that original sin first manifested itself within me. At a very young age I observed my father shaving. It seemed a fairly simple process. After lathering the face with Erasmic by means of bristles from a badger, all one did was to scrape off the whiskers with the razor. What I had not appreciated was that a 'cut-throat' razor was so aptly named. In addition to my throat, fortunately missing the jugular vein, I had lacerated my cheeks and both thumbs. Blood dripped liberally into the wash-basin and onto the floor. On discovery, my mother coated me in talcum powder so that I resembled a cream and jam slice.

Passing quickly over the incident of the sock in the mincing machine, the coal in the lavatory might be worth a mention. Nothing extraordinary about this. For some reason I had decided that it would make good sport to fill the downstairs lavatory with coal. My parents were very happily occupied and unaware that silence had for a few moments prevailed in the house. They had not noticed that I was plying at regular intervals between the coal-scuttle in the dining room and the lavatory via the kitchen. Pretty dexterous with the coal shovel for an eighteen-month old.

I was about six at the time and had acquired a bow and arrow. The bow was of rudimentary construction comprising one of my father's raspberry canes and a piece of hairy string. It had a pull of just a few pounds. For some reason I had determined to shoot a cyclist who was riding along the road on the side close to my house. I crouched behind one of the pair of front gates where I could not possibly be seen by my prey. The wooden gates in the Marlborough Park estate were all identical and of typical 1930's sun-ray design, each gate having a little tulipheadshaped aperture. The tip of the thin green geranium support stake arrow protruded just through the hole in the gate and I was poised with the bow taut. Having held fast until my quarry came into view I closed my eyes and loosed. With my heart racing I opened my eyes expecting to see the poor man lying on his back in the middle of the road with the arrow sticking out of his chest. All I managed to see was the deadly arrow skudding across the surface of the road and no sight at all of the cyclist. I waited in silent horror and deeply remorseful of my intention which, thankfully, I had failed to achieve, when a large shape loomed over the top of the gate and said: "Is this your arrow, Sonny?"

The William pear tree incident has to be reported. Shortly after the move to No. 41, my father had planted a pear tree which by the time I was seven, had matured sufficiently to produce a good crop of fruit. By mid-summer the tree was laden with well formed but rock-hard pears. My father regularly inspected them and, to prevent infestation, he tied a sticky strip around the slim bole. Any ants among the corpses caught by the trap showing signs of movement were dispatched in a tiny wisp of smoke by deftly focussing the sun's rays with a convex lens temporarily removed from my father's binoculars. The boy who lived next door but one was older than me by some five years and it was he, I assert, who lured me into mischief. At his suggestion I was to pick the solid pears one by one, place them in turn on the garden table, which was made of a section of tree trunk, whereupon he was to smash them to smithereens with a croquet mallet. The fiendish plan was executed to perfection, leaving the branches stripped bare and mashed bits of pear strewn over a large area of the lawn. It was an immensely enjoyable half an hour's entertainment. My father was not pleased when he arrived home that evening and sent me straight to bed without my usual nightly *bonne bouche* from his dinner plate. Parents just don't understand us.

The William pear tree as it is today
(scene of crime)

The pens we used, once we had progressed from pencils, comprised a pen-holder and a bronze nib (a Waverley maybe). Pen nibs came in two kinds, there was the stubby bendy kind and the springy kind. They were used with ink which in some schools was made up from what looked like soot mixed with water. An ink monitor would come round the class and fill tiny porcelain ink wells which fitted into a hole in the desk (only on the *right*-hand side of course, right-handedness being *de rigueur*) at the end of a groove designed to retain writing implements. The filthy stuff had a habit of getting all over your fingers and sometimes on clothes. But I digress. It so happened that the tip of said springy sort of nib could be snapped off to form two smaller very sharp tips by means of which it was possible to describe little circles. I thought that the look of my bedroom furniture would be greatly enhanced by decoration so the ends of the bed received the appropriate treatment. The bed head and the foot board each had little circles scored into the French polish at precisely spaced intervals. This left the walnut veneered wardrobe a trifle plain by comparison so its corners were unevenly carved with chamfers by using a small pocket knife which was later confiscated after a serious talking-to. I explained to my father that there was no maliciousness intended on my part, merely artistic expression.

Chapter 7

On becoming a pianist

The popular concert pianists in the forties were Rubinstein, Myra Hess, who performed lunch-time concerts at the National Gallery during the bombing, and Moiseiwitsch. Piano duettists Rawicz and Landauer were heard regularly on the radio and so too was Semprini who broadcast on Sunday nights. I was to emulate none of the above. I was first sent to Mrs Grafton for weekly piano lessons where I struggled to sight read crochets held by smiling elves. All through the lesson Mrs Grafton knitted like Madam Defarge. She could knit without looking. The needles made an infernal racket the entire lesson, as if I didn't have enough to worry about with capricious fingers without having that distraction. She never played a note in all of the year I was with her and I began to think that she couldn't play the piano at all except that there was a certificate on the wall which indicated to the contrary. I somehow achieved Grade 1 for practice and Grade 2 for music theory. Not practising didn't help matters and progress was very slow.

The weekly torture ceased when I was withdrawn from Mrs Grafton's and sent to Miss Phyllis Betts, a charming and more tolerant lady who didn't knit, my parents persisting in the belief that my hidden talent could still be brought to light. Miss Betts lived in North Cray within easy reach by fairy cycle. I rode off each Saturday morning with enthusiasm, not so much for the music lesson which passed off uneventfully, but for the anticipated visit to the blacksmith's in Footscray. I adored the sound of the hammer which he tapped several times on the anvil between each shower of sparks generated as he struck the red-hot metal. With his back to the horse, smoke poured up around him as he placed the red-hot bespoke shoe on the animal's hoof which he held between his knees on the thick leather apron he was wearing. Why did the horse not flinch? I would have. Furthermore, after the final heating and then tempering by dousing the shoe in a tank of water, why did the creature not even bat an eyelid as the shoe was nailed on to his foot? Other boys aspired to be train or bus drivers. I, having seen horses being shod, was determined to be a farrier.

Chapter 8
Park House

My first school was a small private school called Park House situated opposite the war memorial in Sidcup Place past which marched Empire Day parades and later the many Victory Parades. My mother met me in the afternoon of my first day at school and was concerned to find that I had collected an oversized egg on my forehead by slipping over on sand which had spilled from the sand tray.

Within eighteen months I was withdrawn from the school and sent to Cannock House, another small private school, situated in Eltham. This was rather a terrifying experience as all the masters wore black bat gowns and one in particular shouted a great deal. Regular beatings took place reminiscent of scenes from Dickens. On one occasion, following a minor offence for which the culprit failed to own up, the master came round the entire class in turn to inflict punishment. The idea was that each boy lent him his own rule for the exercise and if it broke as it hit the palm of the hand the master would throw a penny on the desk with the instruction to buy a new one. Another time a number of boys were shamed in front of the whole school by being ordered onto the dais one by one and bent over a form whereupon they were given six of the best for nothing more than forming catapults out of mattress springs and pinging paperclips at the girls in the school next door. Fortunately none of the girls was injured. However, it does seem that dumping an old bedstead constructed of hundreds of V-springs in the corner of the playing field was asking for trouble.

At the outbreak of war I was again moved, this time to Lamorbey C of E primary school which was very much more to my liking. To my delight the place was full of very pretty girls and, unlike William Brown, I found invitations to tea after school most agreeable. Not only was there

Lamorbey C of E primary school
('...full of very pretty girls...')

lemonade and cake to look forward to but the chance of a kiss behind the surface air-raid shelter on the way to the young lady's home was an exciting probability. I fell madly in love with one charming creature, a mature seven-year-old. I wrote her name and professions of undying love on the underside of the slate-bedded billiard table beneath which I slept during the raids. My nightly prayers included begging the Almighty to arrange for her home to be bomb-damaged so that I could rescue her from the debris and take her back to the safety of my billiard table where I could cuddle her. Regrettably no answer came from on high and she went out of my life.

At the age of nine I went into the top form, merely by reason of age and not of merit, where I was placed next to a very bright young man who, to me, was a mathematical genius. Just after roll-call and before we had all settled, I was suddenly addressed by the headmistress (Mrs Bolton) who said: "Graham, what is a half of a half?" I don't like questions like that being sprung upon me. I prefer to ponder things carefully and give a considered opinion. A hush came over the class except for the odd snigger, but they all waited in vain, unaware of the mortifying embarrassment I was suffering. She turned away with a pitying look and said: "Tell him, Quentin," and he snapped out the correct answer without hesitation. For years I harboured a grudge against that boy who I believed had so humiliated me. Any blame lay not with him of course. Latterly, in my more mature moments, I have to admit that I very much admire his illustrations in children's books and his radio talks. I haven't seen Quentin Blake since the day I left Lamorbey in December 1941. I look forward to meeting him again.

I was further humiliated by Mrs Bolton when she discovered, by sniffing along the row of children and gradually homing in on me, that I was the guilty party by virtue of having munched my way through a whole bunch of spring onions on the way to school. I thought nothing of it as it seemed a perfectly innocent thing to have done. She made a terrible fuss and ordered the class monitor to open all of the top windows in the room. My punishment was to write out one hundred times the word 'Onion.'

There was one further brush with the same authority following a night of severe bombing. I was on the garage roof with a trowel, replacing the tiles which had been lifted by the blast, when my mother called out to say that I couldn't go to school because it had been damaged in the same raid. At precisely the same time Mrs Bolton was passing the house and about to inform one of the school governors that the school had to close for a few days. Unfortunately for me, she overheard my whoops of joy at my mother's news and accordingly raised the subject of my glee in the following morning assembly. She told everybody how shocked she was that I should be pleased that the school had been damaged and such an attitude was not to be followed by others. I was too tongue-tied to explain that my reaction had been unfairly misinterpreted and that instead of being pleased that the school had been damaged I was overjoyed to have an unexpected holiday.

Chapter 9

'The day war broke out...'

On the Sunday 3rd September 1939, after the wireless bulletin informing us that we were at war, we heard our first heart-stopping wail of the local air-raid siren. The 'all clear' sounded an uneventful hour or so later and someone suggested that a German reconnaissance plane had paid us a visit and had been smartly chased off by our fighter planes. It turned out that it was one of our own aircraft.

The idea that we were going to give the Germans 'what for' seemed great but my mother was in tears as she described to me what a dreadful war had taken place a mere twenty-one years previously. She had been through the Great War as a youngster and had seen the effect on her older brothers as a result of their experiences in the trenches and of the lasting damage to the eyes caused by mustard gas attacks.

My mother's anxiety did not accord with the view taken by the newspapers who gave the impression to me that the impending scrap with the Germans was to be some kind of game. We had a Daily Telegraph map of Europe with all the countries shown in different colours, the United Kingdom being in red, of course, along with the Channel Islands, Gibraltar and Malta. My father explained that we looked after certain areas which were 'ours', like Egypt and Palestine for example and other places which were called 'protectorates'. In addition to the map, the newspaper provided a sheet on which there were printed a goodly number of Union Jacks and few Swastikas. There may have been some French flags but the details escape me. What I do recall is that I was given the job of cutting out all the little flags in pairs and, after applying a squeeze of Seccotine, wrapping each pair around a pin. The map was fixed to a wall in the dining room and the appropriate flags stuck in along the Maginot Line on the French side and along the Siegfried Line on the German side, these 'Lines' comprising overground and underground fortifications built at vast expense extending along opposite sides of the entire border between France and Germany. The 'game' was all set to play and I was ready to start shifting the flags around as the fun proceeded. From the wireless we heard the rousing song: "We're going to hang out the washing on the Siegfried Line, Have you any dirty washing mother dear?"

For quite some time nothing happened to cause any change on the map. We were in what has been termed the 'Phoney War' when both sides on the Western Front were holding off except for the occasional skirmish. Elsewhere there was plenty of activity especially in Poland where the Germans were rapidly advancing. A vast tonnage of shipping was being sunk by German U-boats. The passenger ship Athenia, which had started its voyage before the war, had been sunk the day war was declared.

I have very vivid recollections of two very positive Royal Navy successes which occurred in the early days of the war which cheered us up no end even though they were relatively minor events in the overall scheme of things. In December there was the great sea chase in which the battleship Admiral Graf Spee was cornered in the River Plate, South America. My father explained to me what the word 'scuttle' meant after the German ship had been scuttled i.e. deliberately sunk, by her own sailors on orders from Berlin to avoid the ship being captured by the Navy. The other was the amazing rescue in February 1940 of 299 merchant sailors from the German supply ship Altmark which was hiding in a Norwegian fjord. The seamen had been picked up by the Graf Spee after their ships had been sunk and had been transferred to the Altmark. The cry went up: "The Navy's here!" (I need no reminding) when a boarding party from HMS Cossack opened the Altmark's hatches.

So far as our 'game' was concerned, what we did not know at the time was that the Germans were going to cheat and launch an offensive through Belgium (on the 10th May 1940 to be precise) where there were no flags because Belgium had claimed neutrality. As the Germans advanced through France our flags were being rapidly replaced by Swastikas and the game suddenly became boring. The map and flags were either removed or more likely fell down along with the ceiling plaster when we had our first bomb.

By the end of May, within three weeks, the Germans had advanced to the coast of the Pas de Calais. Held up by much rearguard action and heroism, it was possible to evacuate in the region of 335,000 allied soldiers from the beaches of Dunkirk, often referred to as the 'Miracle of Dunkirk'. The Royal Navy warships and an 'armada' of little ships which included paddle steamers such as the Medway Queen and cabin cruisers manned by bowler-hatted city gents, transported a defeated army across the Straights of Dover to England. It was only a matter of time for the invasion of Britain to start, the first time in nine hundred years apart from a few skirmishes with the Spanish, Dutch and French. In my childlike innocence I was not in the least in awe of the Germans as I had total confidence that eventually we would prevail.

Over a period of several months from September 1939, during the 'Phoney War', we were privileged to enjoy unofficial weekly air displays. In the house backing on to ours lived a young lady whose boyfriend was a pilot. He was a pretty spectacular flyer who turned up overhead with whatever machine he happened to be flying that week. He first performed aerobatics in a Boulton Paul Defiant which had a little turret behind the cockpit for the gunner so made it easy to identify. He, proceeded to 'beat up' his girlfriend's house by diving down to near rooftop height and then circling around waving to his admirers. He came several times in the famous Hawker Hurricane but I suppose what impressed most was the Supermarine Spitfire. With the crackle of its Merlin engine it was the aircraft that fulfilled every schoolboy dream. He flew so low that the distinctive profile of the wings filled the sky and left a lasting impression.

(I cannot resist adding here that many decades later, when holidaying in Cornwall, I was permitted by Nick Grace to have control of his two-seater Spitfire (see below) for just three minutes. For the rest of the flight I endured an aerobatic display of sick-making but exhilarating flying.)

Spitfire Mark IX (ML 407) flown by Carolyn Grace

Chapter 10 '

'The Few'

In August of 1940 the Battle of Britain started in earnest with mass air attacks on airfields, factories and the docks. For me, sitting wide-eyed on the doorstep of the French windows at the rear of the house facing north, the drama being enacted in the sky could not have been more thrilling. Column after black column of German bombers appeared, all flying slowly in a westerly direction over the River Thames towards London. Little black puffs of smoke burst in front of the bombers caused by exploding shells fired from anti-aircraft guns (Ack Ack). Fighter planes made vapour trails in huge swirling patterns as they attacked the bombers and engaged in what I was told were 'dog-fights' with the fighter escort. I saw one plane go down to my right over in the direction of the nearby golf-course. Then another which fell in a vertical dive a few streets to the north of us. I tried to believe that it was not one of ours but I had my doubts because although I hadn't seen the actual impact of the crash I had recognised its profile.

A parachute could be seen over the Eltham area several thousand feet up. I watched it through binoculars as it slowly drifted eastwards until it was enveloped in a pall of black smoke which was rising from a fire in the Erith region. My father said that the pilot would probably have his respirator and should survive. I'm afraid this may have been wishful thinking. Unfortunately, when the noise of the battle had become intense, my mother insisted that I should relinquish my grandstand seat and take cover.

The Battle of Britain lasted for several weeks ending with the rout of the Luftwaffe's campaign to disable the RAF as a prelude to Operation Sealion, the planned German invasion of Britain. The German aircraft were destroyed in their hundreds. On September 15th, which is remembered as Battle of Britain Day, 185 enemy machines were shot down for the loss of 25 of our fighter planes (ten pilots survived). We were encouraged by the stirring words of Winston Churchill who famously said: "Never in human conflict has so much been owed by so many to so few." I had overwhelming confidence in our pilots whom we now refer to as 'The Few.' After that I *knew* that the Germans were going to lose the war. I was quite oblivious of how desperate the situation had been in reality. Operation Sealion was postponed until the following June when it was abandoned in favour of Operation Barbarossa, the offensive against the USSR, to our good fortune.

Not one of 'The Few' but a courageous pilot none-the-less was a Flight Lieutenant I met all too briefly when I was out shopping with my mother in Sidcup, just near the station. I was not normally happy when my mother met up with someone, since my mother liked to chat and at that time there was plenty to chat about. However, on this occasion, here was one of my heroes looking dashing in his smart officer's uniform. His fiancée, Phyllis, held his arm and looked up at him admiringly. Two years later he was shot down when flying a Mosquito over the invasion beaches and was killed. Some twelve months after the tragedy, the former fiancée called in to see my mother. I could see from her sad eyes that Phyllis was a very unhappy lady. She had been many months in a psychiatric ward trying to recover from the loss of her dear friend. After she left our house my mother said to me through her tears: "Did you notice the terrible scar on her neck? She tried to take her own life."

Chapter 11
The Blitz

For me, the Second World War was most stimulating and provided me with so many exciting adventures. The 1987 film 'Hope and Glory' aptly shows, through the eyes of a twelve-year-old, the kind of war I had. Collecting shrapnel (a misnomer to the purist) after a night's raid was good sport especially if you found a big piece with which to impress your chums. A nose cone or better still a whole incendiary bomb would seriously impress. Shrapnel was fascinating stuff, no matter that at 12,000 feet it could be pretty lethal. A fresh piece sparkled and felt slightly prickly in the hand. Between salvos fired from mobile guns shrapnel could be heard pitter-pattering all around like heavy drops of rain. It would have made a mess of anyone standing underneath after falling from that height. Hence, on the night I was carried to safety from our shattered house, I wore my toy tin hat on top of my school cap to give me complete security, so I thought.

The hundreds of barrage balloons over London and the suburbs were a great comfort. They were supposed to protect us from dive-bombers, provided that the winch crews got them up in time. Not everyone approved; a few strange folk complained that the balloons were causing visual pollution. I did see one balloon that had slipped its moorings and watched it until it was a mere speck in the sky which, incidentally, was completely blue, except for a confusion of vapour trails. My father reassured me that one of our pilots would be sent up to shoot it down. He took me to see a winch operating in a recreation ground in Blackfen where a group of onlookers stood around to see the huge silvery giant of a thing safely winched in. Bits of balloon material were another collectors' item.

The bombing raids, which were called the 'Blitz', took place between September 1940 and May 1941 and between January to June 1944. There were more than 120 heavy raids over London and the South-east during the first period. We got used to the nightly wail of the siren and took shelter to await the start of the bombardment. It wasn't long before we could hear the sinister drone of the German bombers and then the anti-aircraft batteries opening up. The noise was intense. The bombs shrieked and the explosions shook the house so that everything rattled. The mobile anti-aircraft guns close by, I think Bofors, made a rapid 'pip, pip, pip' sound echoing all around.

The bomb which fell from the sky one night in 1941 made a terrifying swishing sound increasing in intensity as it descended, ending with a huge explosion which caused temporary deafness due to the pressure wave that it created. Once the crashing of falling tiles and broken windows had stopped there was an eerie silence except for the constant muffled crump, crump of gun-fire. The bomb fell in a garden in the middle of our block. It was one of a 'stick of bombs' which straddled the Marlborough Park area. I was satisfied with the explanation that Germans were so frightened by the barrage which our anti-aircraft batteries were putting up that they simply jettisoned their bombs and headed off for home.

At the moment the bomb fell, my father had been on his way to the ambulance station wearing his tin hat on which he had painted the letters 'FA' (for 'first aid'). We deliberately interpreted the initials as 'Football Association' to his annoyance. As soon as he heard the swishing sound it didn't take him long to dive for cover behind the front wall of a house in Marlborough Park Avenue. A quick assessment satisfied him that the family were safe (which later brought a snort from my mother), he made his way by a direct route, since there were no fences left upright, to where the bomb had fallen to find a large crater a few feet away from an Anderson shelter. At the entrance was a policeman who was in a state of shock having just survived the bomb himself and moreover having discovered an injured boy in the shelter. My father more or less brushed the poor man aside and found the boy lying on a camp bed in extreme pain and bleeding as a result of a large piece of bomb casing embedded in his chest. He also had a small piece in his left wrist which was bleeding profusely. He bandaged the boy's chest after cutting off his pyjama top and applied a tourniquet to the upper part of the arm and a bandage to the wound. He tied a label on the boy to indicate the starting time of compression of the artery. The ambulance team soon arrived and the boy was taken to Queen Mary's hospital for an operation and, satisfyingly for all concerned, a full recovery.

I am confident that it was the boy's *left* arm that was injured as I went to the hospital with my father and can still visualise the bedside scene with my father looking at the fast healing wound and joking that there might still be a piece of shrapnel left in the wrist which he would gladly fish out with his pocket knife. My father was congratulated by the nursing staff for the efficiency of his first aid which was evidently of a better quality than his joke.

By the time the V1s appeared in 1944 my father had been given a smart dark blue uniform complete with Light Rescue shoulder flashes. In the early part of the war he had acted in a freelance capacity as he was highly qualified in First Aid. He saw no point in sitting at the command centre when no warning had sounded but would immediately turn up for duty the moment the anti-aircraft guns opened up on the German bombers.

The scene the following morning can easily be imagined as, regrettably, there have recently been plenty of reminders of devastation coming to us on our TV screens. Clearing up the mess of bomb damage was a procedure to which we became well versed by the end of the war. I became proficient at tiling which involved re-seating the tiles so that the nibs once more hooked over the roof battens. The shards of glass covering the furniture and carpets I left to my parents. Some windows remained intact, helped by a covering of netting. The gardens had been laid waste. The fences were match-wood, though some chestnut palings still remained. The top of a flag-pole in the garden where the bomb had fallen, was missing. Neighbours said that the bomb had struck the flag-pole just before landing. The extending ladders in the garage, which I have to this day, had holes through the side cheeks showing the devastating effect of shrapnel. The houses along one side of the block were so severely damaged that they had to be vacated.

These houses offered new territory for exploration, especially as there were no doors left on their hinges. No matter that many poor souls had lost all their possessions or may have been injured, here we children had the world at our feet. Easily led by some older boys (who else ?) I joined a gang of marauders who went from house to house destroying anything which had survived the blast. The remains of dining-room pendant light fittings were easy pickings, their three upturned frosted glass shades being speedily dispatched with the swing of an axe. Panes of glass disintegrated under a hail of well-aimed pieces of roof-tile which were abundantly available as ammunition, crunching underfoot as we surged from room to room. Any windows which were protected with tapes in Union Jack pattern or sheets of muslin, deserved special attention. A tile projected at high velocity would make a very satisfying neat rectangular hole in a window pane so protected. One of our number had a penchant for telephones as he severed the wires with a single blow, though what he intended to do with them remained a mystery. I have to admit to a feeling of unease as our gang hacked a path of additional destruction through what a few days before had been peoples' homes. The more we progressed unimpeded, the more a feeling of freedom from authority asserted itself within the psyche. We became indomitable and beyond the law. My present day thoughts are that the lot of us should have been wheeled off to a remand home. But the war does funny things to people......

On a lone sortie I investigated the remains of our neighbour's sheet asbestos potting-shed which had sagged at a precarious angle. Mr Harper, an elderly gentleman who had already removed to the West Country, had used it for a quiet pipe as he had been debarred from smoking in the house. Amongst the paraphernalia of broken flower pots and gardening tools I discovered a particularly attractive pot which was shaped like an inkwell but was many times larger than an inkwell. I immediately termed it a 'Flowerpot-Inkwell' and announced it as such on presenting it to my mother. I was most offended by her response. "Take that filthy thing away," she yelled. "It's a Flowerpot-Inkwell," I persisted. "Take it back at once!" she ordered. I was only nine, how was I to know what a spittoon was ?

Chapter 12

The 'Operation'

My Uncle Frank worked in SE London for the gas company and had not been called up into the army as his job was considered to be a 'reserved occupation'. On one of his days off, he arrived at our house to make a start on the Anderson shelter in the back garden. Now I come to think of it, it wasn't strictly an Anderson shelter that was built but a creation designed by my father who had not hung about waiting for the men from the council to deliver the materials and instead had bought a number of corrugated iron sheets along with a stack of hefty timber from the South London Iron Company.

I watched with interest as the hole in the flowerbed grew. At a depth of about six feet my uncle placed the first sheet across part of the hole and, working backwards, dug out more and more soil which he piled up onto the sheet. To my horror the whole thing caved in under the weight of soil and he narrowly escaped being buried. It was eventually completed, my father over-engineering the construction with the baulks of wood supporting several tonnes of soil on top.

The family spent many nights in this home-made shelter during the first few weeks of heavy bombing. We also spent many nights when nothing happened so that the shelter was abandoned in favour of sleeping under the billiard table which had been dragged to a position under the stairs, the hefty oak sideboard having been moved to close off the makeshift indoor shelter.

Interspersed with the bombing we were receiving, the RAF were making night raids on targets in Germany. I was quite convinced that the RAF bombers such as Stirlings, Whitleys and Wellingtons, and later the Lancasters, all made a friendly humming sound unlike the Luftwaffe's Dorniers, Heinkels and Messerschmitts which had engines which characteristically throbbed threateningly. I tried to put to the back of my mind the fact that many lives were being lost. I prayed fervently for the airmen to be kept safe. I willed our bombers to return without loss and listened to the morning news bulletin hoping to hear the words from Alvar Liddell that "...all of our aircraft have returned safely."

Now, being a fairly inventive sort of person, even at the age of nine, I found another use for the redundant garden air-raid shelter. It was my secret den! This is where I invited my friends to play and to have daytime feasts after school. It was in this very shelter that I performed my first 'operation' on the girl next door during a lull in the bombing. We were playing 'doctors and nurses' and Betty was lying full length on the camp bed with her tummy exposed. The moment was fast approaching when I was to take the first big decision in my young life which was to establish me as a person of authority.

The operation was being performed with an open nappy pin serving as a scalpel. Scratching along her delicate skin to add authenticity, I had reached a crucial position of the progressing 'incision'. Travelling south, I had arrived at a region beyond her navel when I realised that a certain piece of elastic tape of her undergarment would impede successful completion of the cut adequate to access the offending organ. Being a little boy of some breeding I asked my patient: "Do I take your knickers down?" to which she replied tartly: "You're the *doctor* - you decide!"

Chapter 13

Bombed out!

We were to survive several bombings, the second causing a similar mess as in the first. As before, the men from the council came and nailed translucent strips across the windows until the glass could be replaced. The third bomb, which fell close by, shook the walls so violently that large cracks formed in the main supporting walls. Over the mattress where my sister was sleeping, a large chunk of plaster had come away from the wall and hung by a thin strip of wallpaper. The French windows, complete with window frame, were lying across the flower bed so that the dining room was completely exposed, the still swinging centre light fitting being silhouetted against flashes of gunfire and a fan of searchlights. With my eyes filled with dust and my hair matted with plaster I stood up in the darkness and immediately impaled my foot on a sliver of glass which had ended up on the floor leaning at a steep angle against the edge of the mattress. This called for a stiff upper lip as I removed the glass which was sticking out through my blood-soaked bed-sock. Not until I caught sight of my Bren-gun carrier and lead soldiers which had been demolished, did I burst into tears and sob my opinion of Hitler.

An assessment of the damage confirmed that our house was no longer habitable. My father arranged to rent a large six-bedroomed mock-Tudor house in Christchurch Road (on the corner with Priestlands Park Road) where we were to remain throughout the war and for a further two years. It had a large garden with two excellent trees suitable for climbing, one being conveniently forked to support a tree house, the other having a handy horizontal branch about twenty feet up over which I could hook my legs and hang upside down like a bat. This habit didn't meet with my mother's approval.

The house itself had two main attractions for me. One was an eaves loft which I appropriated as a workshop where I had a treadle lathe, a bench for model-making and a vivarium for my butterflies and moths. The second was the sloping roof accessible at a fairly low level by climbing onto the top of the potting shed situated at the rear of the house. The roof led up to a pitched roof, the apex of which ran fore and aft of the house. I shall return to the matter of this splendid roof at the end of my story.

The gable on which I sat on VE-Day

We kept hens at the bottom of the garden as we were encouraged to do by Lord Woolton of the Ministry of Food. My Saturday morning job was to clean out the chicken house, the straw and droppings serving as fertilizer for the vegetable patch. We were never short of a bird for the table. After nominating which poor creature's neck was to be rung I would keep out of the way until the deed was done. I was glad I did so because my father told me that much to his horror on his first attempt at killing a chicken he had pulled its head right off! I don't think my mother actually relished the idea of putting her hand inside the carcass to draw out its entrails but she did so none the less. As a 'towny' I was not enamoured of the whole messy business. However, any sympathy I might have had for the sacrificial hen quickly evaporated once the resulting delicious dish was placed before me.

The plot of land next to our house was requisitioned for use by the National Fire Service (NFS) formerly the Auxiliary Fire Service (AFS). A large brick-built reservoir was constructed and filled with water. The barbed-wire protective fence along the top of the brickwork proved little resistance to a group of ice-hockey enthusiasts when a sufficient thickness of ice had formed. We borrowed the girls' hockey sticks and used an Action Ration tin for a puck. (Action Rations were tablets of compressed malt issued by the School tuck-shop and were probably Horlicks tablets.)

I had heard my mother talk about soldiers from the Great War suffering from shell-shock. It meant little until, rather alarmingly, I witnessed for myself the effect upon a sufferer. Following the fourth time we lost all the windows, the council men arrived yet again to cover up the windows with whatever materials were available. One man was working at the rear of the house when there was a thunderous explosion nearby. Being more or less inured to the sound of gunfire and bombs after five years of war, I took little notice of the event whereas the workman threw himself into our back porch where he cowered and trembled violently for several minutes covering his head and face with his hands. I stood over him and could see that he was severely distressed and so immediately called my mother who instantly recognised the symptoms. She reassured him that the danger had passed and he gradually recovered with the comfort of a cigarette and a cup of tea. I was most concerned for the poor fellow.

Chapter 14
DYB DYB DYB

I joined the 3rd Sidcup Wolf Cub Pack at the age of nine and took to the Baden Powell movement with much more enthusiasm than I did school. In the Cubs I teamed up with Ron Skinner who has been a staunch friend ever since. I excelled at British Bulldog and In The River-On The Bank, Kim's game and practical things like knots and first aid. Proficiency badges were obtained by external examination on presenting a piece of handicraft to a suitably qualified person for inspection together with an interview. On presentation of my half made rug which was the result of many onerous hours hooking little lengths of folded over wool onto a hessian backing, the lady examiner informed me that the rules for qualification called for the article to be a finished one. This took me aback for a moment until a thought struck me and I earnestly pleaded in mitigation that there was a war on, in case she had forgotten, and ready cut wool was very difficult to obtain. I think she awarded the badge more for effrontery than for quality of craftsmanship.

Within a year I had progressed to the rank of Sixer and was asked to lead my six in a district competition called the Barham Trophy. This was held at the headquarters of another pack which met in a hall in Grassington Road , now the site of a new Safeway supermarket. After an afternoon of tests our pack was adjudged the winner. To round off the day, all the packs formed a circle with ours in the middle. Everybody came to attention and waited in silence for a signal for the start of the presentation ceremony. There was a long pause and nobody moved until I realised that it was up to me to start proceedings which I did by yelling at the top of my voice: "DYB DYB DYB" to which the whole assembly chorused: "We'll DOB DOB DOB!" (Do Your Best/ Do Our Best)

Akela had organised an afternoon on Chislehurst Common and

had informed the pack that we were to meet at 2.30 by the 228 bus-stop opposite the War Memorial. We would then proceed to a clearing in the woods where we would play rounders and finish up with a picnic. I waited for my fellow cubs to arrive but none came. Ever optimistic, I stayed doggedly at my post for the best part of two hours anxiously looking for those green caps with yellow piping. None came. It so happened that it had been raining throughout the afternoon but not in my judgment enough to warrant cancellation, not at least for one of stout heart.

Bitterly disappointed, I returned home with my Shipham's fish-paste sandwiches and burst into tears the moment my mother opened the front door. A phone call ascertained that the rest of the wolf cub pack had had a party in the warmth of Akela's home as had been agreed in the event of rain. More tears.

Chapter 15

Big school

To my parents' delight I succeeded in passing the entrance exam to the junior school of Eltham College (School for the Sons of Missionaries) and started my 'big' school on the 14th January 1942. The first name I soon became familiar with was that of Eric Liddell, a Scottish missionary's son who himself became a missionary in China, although he may be better known as the 400 metre gold medallist in the 1924 Olympic Games held in Paris. His great sporting battle against Harold Abrahams is the subject of the film 'Chariots of Fire' made in 1981. In 1945 we all stood in silence in Chapel when the headmaster announced that he had died in a Japanese prisoner of war camp.

On my first morning at Eltham I joined a group of boys at Sidcup station all well wrapped up against a freezing cold day in their new caps, scarves, and socks with the tops turned over bearing the school colours. Our trousers and raincoats were all bought a size too big on the premise that we would 'soon grow into them.' We all carried gas-masks. I kept mine in a metal cylinder which had a lid held securely by two snap clips in a similar manner to the now obsolete Bakelite distributor head. I never went without my gas-mask. It became my talisman, evidently with proven qualities.

It was an easy journey from Sidcup to Mottingham, just two stops on the train. On arriving at Mottingham station we were confronted by the spectacle of Smoky Joe. Much has been written about this extraordinary tramp whose real name was George Curnow. He lived up to his name as he wore the filthiest clothes and had frayed knitted mittens from the ends of which protruded grimy fingers holding a mouth-organ. Against the railings bordering the alleyway leading from the exit to the main road, he lent his bicycle which was without tyres and chain. From the handlebars he hung a can of smoking coals to enable him to warm his hands between musical numbers. He wasn't very good tempered, well not with us anyway, and so growled at us as we cheerily greeted him in the mornings. It was said that the police took him in once a month to give him a bath which doesn't bear further conjecture. Also, so the story goes, he came from a wealthy family who had disowned him. We never did learn the exact truth.

Smoky Joe

My first experience of collective schoolboy mentality came to me in the ritualistic vandalism carried out on the train which must have cost the Southern Railway a small fortune in electric light bulbs as they were gleefully hurled out of the window onto the lines. This destruction was soon ended once the distinctive royal blue caps with gold Maltese crosses were recognised by the people whose gardens backed on to the railway. My gas-mask disappeared during one of the journeys during the first week only to be found in the nick of time hanging from the carriage door-handle on the outside of the train.

Joan Brown was my first teacher at Eltham College. She was the kindest of people, the daughter of a couple who served in India under the aegis of the London Missionary Society and as a consequence she had been a boarder at Walthamstow Hall, Sevenoaks, the sister school to Eltham College. She once told me the story of how she circumvented the strict rules, which banned playing on Sundays, by lining up her dolls in a row and reading the Bible to them. It was said that she had been bereaved by the loss of her fiancé early in the war but we were unaware of this at the time. I kept in touch with her practically every year until she died just a few years ago at the age of ninety-seven.

Other boys who joined at that time were John Willes, mentioned above, Doug Thompson and Douglas Crabb whose name caused a snigger around the class until silenced by Miss Brown. Another boy who had joined in the September term before me was Michael Saward, recently retired Canon of St. Paul's Cathedral. I should have known that he would do well as a leader the moment he was singled out to be Pharoah in the end of term form play. I, on the other hand, was clearly not regarded as leadership material and was given the less taxing job of a slave who kept Pharoah cool in the Egyptian heat by fanning him with a shrimping net.

In the first week after the beginning of my first term we were taken to the senior school gymnasium. After the usual formal exercises and team relays, the PT master (latterly PE) introduced us to Monkeys' Paradise. He directed the boys to hook forms at an incline to the wall bars and to beams which were lowered from the ceiling. Mats were dragged from the corner of the room for distribution around the floor as 'islands' and thick climbing ropes hanging from a rail attached to the ceiling were drawn from the sides to serve as vines. One boy was chosen to wear a coloured band and he would attempt to catch the others who would flee in all directions through the trees in the jungle, swinging on the vines and scampering around trying not to fall off the islands into the water. It was nothing more than a grand game of 'He', but immensely exciting.

Eltham College and Britain's largest plane tree

Not so exciting was our first swimming lesson in the school bath, formerly the old gym as evidenced by the rusty hooks in the cross beams in the roof structure. Now, before I explain this excruciating episode of my life, it must be understood that I was brought up in a home where things lavatorial or matters concerning reproduction were not given a mention. When my father went to the lavatory (we didn't say toilet) I was forbidden to speak to him. I had to pretend for a brief moment that he simply didn't exist. As to our nether regions, no reference was made other than my mother telling me to 'look after yourself' and to 'wash yourself carefully.' Hence, at the age of ten I was deeply conscious of the fact that I must not be 'seen.' (The reader will by now realise that I have described this aspect of my upbringing without the use of any unacceptable anatomical terms which to this day are still repugnant to me!)

So it was with utter horror that the whole class was lined up not just naked but *stark* naked along the poolside for our first lesson. As we were spread out along one end and an adjacent side of the bath, the two lines of male nudes were effectively facing each other across the pool so that we had no choice other than to make comparisons of what passed as our manhood. From that moment on, each boy was identified as a Roundhead or a Cavalier. Furthermore, I was appalled by the gross figure of the master instructing us, similarly unattired, who seemed to have hair growing all over his body, in some places somewhat excessively I thought.

The lesson started with everybody sitting on the cold stone bath surround and splashing about with our legs. It was explained that this activity was to drive to the far end of the bath all the spiders and earwigs, which had fallen in the night from the rafters onto the surface of the water. We somehow learnt to swim.

In the summer of 1942 we had athletics. Sports Day was to be held at the end of term. Expectations of me ran high because it was discovered that I could run fast for my age. I won both heats and was in the final of the 80 yards junior sprint. Came the great day and with my hopes high, my parents arrived to cheer me on. My father brought with him his 9.5 mm cine camera (today's camcorder), which may well have been bought specially for the occasion. He stood at the finishing line ready to witness for posterity my glorious success as I breasted the tape.

Alas, it didn't quite work out as I had hoped. I was new to athletics and had not had the experience of a starting pistol. The gun went off with a frightening report. I didn't move off the starting line. It was as though I had been shot. By the time I realised that I ought to be running I could see the backs of the other runners several yards down the track. I gave chase and came in fourth.

My glorious failure remains recorded on film which lies buried, along with my pride, in the family archives. I think the winner was Denis Bews who some fifteen years later was my best man.

Chapter 16

'Macky'

Our art master was an exceedingly talented man. He had several foolproof methods of maintaining discipline. It was really quite simple and most effective. As we were arranged with our easels facing inwards it was not possible to judge when an assault was to take place as he strolled around behind us to inspect our paintings. If twisting an ear failed to bring results he would resort to applying a pincer-like grip to a fold of your neck and giving that a slow turn. The pain was excruciating so it worked every time. Apart from a severe earache or leaving red weals on one's neck there was little harm done. All the class laughed as the victim underwent the ordeal so it was accepted as jolly good harmless fun.

Despite the occasional bouts of torture, Mr. McIver otherwise gave us superb instruction in watercolour painting. With a flick of his brush he could turn disaster into an acceptable piece of artwork. He ran the school puppet club. The first puppet show I saw in my first year at Eltham was his production entitled 'Fairy Hall' which I gather is what the main building of Eltham College was originally called. A luminous skeleton rattled about the stage as *Danse Macabre* was played, its legs and arms being choreographed to disengage from the body and reassemble according to the music. The finale of the turn was the disappearance of the skeleton's skull as it shot up behind the prescenium arch leaving behind a pile of bones. We yelled with delight. The following year saw a performance of the 'Little Mermaid' in which shoals of fish traversed the stage and an octopus popped his head out of a pot lying on the sea-bed. Later when I joined the puppet club we put on 'Jack and the Beanstalk' in which a goose laid a golden egg and a cow produced milk by pumping its tail. Arthur Wyatt (recently retired surgeon), who had a nice treble voice, was detailed to sing 'Heigh-ho! Come to the fair'.

From the sixties onward I regularly visited Macky with my family at his home in Moniaive, Dumfriesshire. The children took it in turns to throw a pot on his wheel under the guidance of his firm hands known all too well to me. He recounted one interesting story of many and that concerned Mervyn Peake, the author of 'Gormenghast.' Peake was a boarder at Eltham during the thirties and by all accounts was an individualist. Above his bed in the dormitory he had painted a mural of nude ladies with, as Macky described in his Scottish accent, "huge brrreasts." Matron complained and the Headmaster, outraged , asked for the art master's opinion as to whether the mural was art or pornography. "A bit of both, sir," came the reply; "I would suggest, sir, that to expel the boy would result in a great loss of talent to the school." Fortunately, his advice was heeded.

Chapter 17

Close encounters

In September of 1942 I went into Miss Jones' form. She was also a very pleasant lady and always allowed me freedom of expression especially when acting extempore to demonstrate a particular adjective. In my enthusiasm, to give my interpretation of being intoxicated, I was prepared to risk injury to impress my classmates by bringing the piano lid down on my fingers, but, with good reason, I was thwarted by Miss Jones' intervention.

In January 1943 I came closer to the enemy than I could have possibly imagined. Our game of quad soccer was interrupted by the sound of aircraft coming towards the school at great speed and with increasing volume. I looked up to see a plane coming directly over the school tower, so low in fact that I could see the pilot's face and the black cross insignia on the port side of the fuselage which gave a clear indication that this aircraft was decidedly not one of ours. Whilst my ability to identify aircraft at the age of ten was quite good I wasn't going to loiter to satisfy my pride. With a unison cry of "It's a Jerry!" we rushed towards the cloister shelter. Not a soul managed to get into the shelter first try but instead we ended up at the entrance as a huge heap of wriggling boys.

We learned later that we had been extremely fortunate in that the flight of Focke-Wulf 190s had not paid attention to our school. Instead they had carried on to Catford and had bombed Sandhurst Road school with the loss of three teachers and fifty children. They also straffed the streets with canon-fire, killing a baby in a pram and the mother. Some excuses have been offered in mitigation of this appalling act of terror upon civilians by suggesting that the target had been the Hither Green marshalling yards but from the many eye-witness accounts the attack was evidently callously deliberate.

*'I looked up to see a plane coming directly over
the school tower...'*

Leaping forwards sixty years for a moment, it was extraordinary to discover only recently from my opposite neighbour, whom I have known for thirteen years, that she had been a pupil at Sandhurst Road on the day of the attack. She walked home to lunch as was her habit but on her return for afternoon classes arrived to find her school destroyed along with several of her friends.

My time in Upper 1 was relatively uneventful apart from the FW190 event I have just described and I was grateful that Miss Jones had encouraged me sufficiently to ensure that I was allowed to continue at Eltham in the senior school provided that my father was willing to pay the hefty fees (all of twelve guineas a term at that time) as I had failed the 11+ which I put down to the examiners having had an off day.

My second encounter with the enemy was when I was cycling along a country lane in the region of Crocken Hill just beyond Orpington. I was awakened from my reverie by the sound of voices from a nearby orchard. A group of smiling and laughing workers called out to me in a gutteral language and as we all know it is to the German language that that adjective is peculiarly applied. What these prisoners of war had to be jolly about, except possibly that for them their fighting was over, I was not too sure. They called to me and waved. I waved politely in return and cycled on hurriedly, astonished at what I had seen.

Chapter 18

V1s and V2s

The first few months of 1944 were relatively calm apart from the occasional air-raid warning which strangely no longer caused your heart to miss a beat as it did at the start of the war. The Allies were gradually pushing the battlefront northwards in Italy. At home the invasion fleet and Mulberry Harbour were being made ready in various ports all around southern England.

Then not long after the Normandy landings on D-Day June 6th, a new sound was to be heard in the skies over Kent. The flying bombs, soon euphemistically renamed 'Doodle-bugs,' arrived at frequent intervals with what became a recognisably very loud clatter caused by the high-speed oscillating metal flap in the pulse-jet propulsion unit which pushed the pilotless craft along at speeds in excess of 350 mph.

Provided that the engine kept going it was possible to be fairly blasé. I even ran out into the garden as they approached to watch them pass overhead. The time to worry was when the engine cut out, always abruptly and seemingly with a final roar, which was followed by a terrifying few seconds of silence until the inevitable deafening explosion. The sound of a 2000lb warhead exploding had several effects upon you. In addition to being shaken up by the blast you were left with successive feelings of relief and elation on realising that you were still in one piece.

From a tree-house which my school friend Vernon Sharpington and I had built in a tall elm in his garden in Leas Green, Chislehurst, we watched the progress of a Doodle-bug flying very fast from the direction of Swanley. As it came up on Sidcup the engine stopped and we saw the machine nose-dive at a steep angle to the ground. The explosion, which we heard one or two seconds later, sent up a column of smoke. It had landed in Old Farm Avenue, destroying some houses and causing a number of fatalities.

My father was on business in Poole on the night a number of flying bombs fell in our area. One made a direct hit on the ambulance station in Marlborough Park Avenue where my father usually met up with his team of light rescue volunteers. Three lives were lost and all of the ambulances totally destroyed. When my father phoned to ask if everything was all right my mother was at a loss to explain over the phone about the ambulance station and that our house had once again been damaged, for fear of giving away vital information to the enemy, because of her awareness that 'Careless talk costs lives' (a Government interdiction which had been much publicised on the radio and by the cartoonist Fougasse).

The flying bombs were then joined by Hitler's second terror weapon, the V2 rockets (which incidentally had been designed by Werner von Braun who headed the Saturn rocket team which enabled the Americans to land on the Moon). I didn't actually see any rockets arrive as they travelled at over 2000mph but I heard plenty of them and I saw the trail of one, left behind as it carved a hole vertically down through the clouds. There was a fearsome bang and I instinctively threw myself under a bush, though little protection that would have given me! It had come down in Days Lane, Sidcup, a mile and a half away from where I lived, causing more devastation and loss of life.

I counted the number of V1s I had seen and had clocked up the grand score of 22 when my father decided that the situation had become unacceptably dangerous for the family and that we should all be evacuated.

Chapter 19

The Evacuee.

My brother Nicholas was conceived during the Blitz. His arrival in July 1941 went more or less unnoticed by me as at that time I was preoccupied with my friends and enjoying the entertainment that the war was providing. The poor child was issued with a respirator which looked like a spaceman's helmet from early science fiction films. It completely enclosed his body except for his legs which kicked furiously to register disapproval. My sister was given a respirator which was called a 'Mickey Mouse' gas-mask, so-called to appease the wearer, although it looked nothing like the familiar character.

Unlike many thousands of children who were officially labelled up and sent off to billets all around the country, some abroad sadly never to return, my father had arranged for me to be evacuated privately. My mother, sister and brother went to stay with two elderly sisters (probably in their fifties!) who shared a house in Worsley. The ladies were obliged to do their bit for the war effort and having had their names on the authorities' list were accordingly asked to take in the evacuee family. My mother said that the set-up was reminiscent of 'Arsenic and Old Lace.' The house was a minefield so far as children were concerned as the tables and mantelpieces were laden with knick-knacks. She lived in fear of the children breaking anything or spilling their milk on the Wilton, so they spent most of each day either in the nearby park or more often in the local cinema in which, being fairly empty in the afternoons, she could relax while my brother, who was never without his silver ARP (Air Raid Precautions) badge, played in the aisle with his cars. It must have been a very anxious time for my mother for although my father was not away in the army, as many thousands of young husbands were, she rarely saw him as he stayed on in the London area all through the V1 and V2 bombardment and continued to serve in the Light Rescue as he had done throughout the Blitz.

I was packed off to stay once more with the Slaughter family which by then included David. They had rented a cottage in Whiteleaf, Buckinghamshire. I was by this time twelve years old and found myself in a rural environment quite unknown to me. There was so much to see and investigate life was anything but dull. The countryside was idyllic and peaceful. People spoke in a local accent which I found so appealing that I tried to emulate their vowel sounds but only managed to make the word 'cow' marginally convincing.

Mr Slaughter, a keen flyer before the war, volunteered for the Royal Air Force and served in the meteorology section in London with the rank of squadron leader. On the evenings it was learnt that he would be home on leave there was a general buzz of excitement as the children awaited their father's arrival.

Evacuated Child: " What, you ain't got no sirens or doodle-bugs! It must be very dull here."

At bedtime I frequently volunteered to make the girls their nightcap of Bournville cocoa. I had perfected the art of cocoa-making, or so I thought, and offered the girls a choice of cocoa with bubbles on the surface or without. It was simply a matter of how the National Dried Milk was first mixed with the cocoa. All went well for several weeks as they thought bubbles to be rather nice. What possessed the younger girl to throw out a challenge to my expertise and ask for cocoa without bubbles I can't think. Needless to say, she did and the wretched bubbles appeared despite use of the appropriate formula. Thus occurred the first blow to my self-esteem delivered by those little pests.

During one of my cocoa duties, I was foolish enough to lift the lid of the kettle for the purpose of re-filling. The steam caused large blisters to come up on the backs of my knuckles which was extremely painful. In an attempt to distract my mind from the agony, I ran around the garden several dozen times. That didn't help, so I retired hurt to my summer-house in the garden where I managed to sleep the night with my sore hand in an enamel jug full of cold water. This little experience served as a simple physics lesson on the subject of latent heat.

My bedroom, which I had to myself, was perfectly comfortable although I preferred to sleep in the summer-house which I made my domain. Here, beside my camp bed, I kept my art equipment and wood-working tools. A cardboard box contained bits of model aeroplane, a few lengths of balsawood, Gillette razor blades and a tube of balsawood cement. I also had a few books including the Ian Allen train spotters' and aircraft spotters' publications; I had spotted all forty 'Schools Class' Southern Railway locomotives with the exception of Eton which I am pleased to say I saw passing through London Bridge six years later.

I made young David a railway station from pieces of three-ply wood. The trim along the platform roof had a series of V-notches just as I remembered I had seen at Sidcup station. I was a trifle smug about that. The non-skid surface of the platform *per se* was a novel mix of sand and paint. Little stickers advertising 'Players Please, it's the tobacco that counts' and 'Virol for anaemic girls' were applied to the back wall to add reality.

Mary was not anaemic. Far from it, she was a very attractive ten-year-old with whom I fell in love the day of my arrival. She had forgotten the incident of my pouring hot water on her back when she was five. I dearly wanted to go for walks with her by ourselves but no matter what subterfuge I devised, her sister Judith would persist in playing gooseberry. When I suggested to her mother that I would like to go for a walk in the woods with Mary, her mother obligingly agreed and arranged for the rest of the family to go too. The walk turned out to be a personal disaster for me as will become evident.

The Whiteleaf cottage stood in a tree-lined countryside lane and was surrounded by lawns and apple trees. One warm afternoon I was sitting in the front garden sketching an apple tree when an elderly gentleman looked over the hedge. He introduced himself and asked if he could see how I was progressing. He made some kindly comments of encouragement and then asked me if I would like to go with him along the lane to his home as he too was an artist and would like to show me his paintings. In those days paedophiles had not been invented or at least they were not prevalent so our young minds were not filled with the dire warnings children are bombarded with in present times.

Looking up at him as we strolled slowly up the lane, I deferred to his superior knowledge on the subject of art and interjected, when appropriate, as knowledgeably as I could. Passing through his beautifully manicured garden, he led me into the kitchen and introduced me to his wife by saying: "Look, my dear, I've found a young artist." I recall the words verbatim just as they were uttered all those years ago. I was a little embarrassed though very proud to have been referred to as an artist but I went along with it with an air of modesty. After explaining the circumstances of my arrival in Whiteleaf, he took me into the lounge to show me his watercolours. These were hunting scenes and all painted with an exceptionally high standard of draftsmanship. The years with Mr McIver had taught me enough to recognise the skill involved in their production.

In one scene he had included a horse and rider moving, as it were, away from the onlooker. He was at pains to point out that although he had not included the horse's head in the painting, none the less, one could see the horse's head in the mind's eye since the rider was depicted leaning towards the horse's neck and he held reins which extended towards the unseen bridle where they evidently ended. At first I didn't quite follow what he was getting at and bluffed by putting on an earnest expression which left little room for raising the level of demonstrating comprehension once I had twigged. It was an uplifting experience being with that charming couple. After accepting a cup of tea and thanking them for such an interesting time, without overdoing the effusiveness, I returned down the lane in high spirits. Further attempts at sketching were made indoors where I would not be spotted. The strain of a similar encounter would have been too much.

By good fortune, I found in the garage a 26-inch-wheel bicycle. The tyres were flat but not perished and the saddle was too high. In no time at all I had it ready to try out only to find that it had a fixed wheel. This took some getting used to but with practice I soon mastered the technique and off I rode to cover many miles through the Buckinghamshire and Oxfordshire countryside. I would be gone for the whole day with no-one to be concerned provided that I reappeared for dinner. Many of the main roads had cycle paths, which, although weed-covered, made for safe riding.

As I was travelling towards Aylesbury one afternoon enjoying my new found freedom, I heard an aircraft. There was always plenty of aerial activity going on so I paid little attention for a while until I realised that I had not heard one like this. I dismounted and waited. It was not long before the aircraft came into view. The sight was awesome. It was flying, very slowly, at an altitude of not much over a few hundred feet. There were holes all over the fuselage and wings. Two of the propellers were not rotating as they should have been, they had been 'feathered'. It was unmistakably a B17 Flying Fortress of the USAAF which was limping back to somewhere like Brize Norton, I supposed, after having been on a daylight raid over Germany. I watched in amazement as it struggled through the air and thought about what the airmen had just been suffering. I watched it until it was out of sight and willed it on its way. There's not much else a schoolboy can do in such circumstances.

I rode on to Aylesbury into the centre of town. I found a sweetshop and propped my bike against the kerb, easy to do with a fixed wheel. As I was about to cross the pavement I saw rolling towards me a shilling coin (5p). It described a spiral path and ended up at my feet and coincidentally in front of two very large feet which, as I looked up, I discovered belonged to a very large policeman. I picked up the coin with the intention of handing it to him but before I raised my hand to offer what I knew did not belong to me he said: "I would put that in your pocket if I were you." What luck! I took his advice. However, it soon went on a bottle of Tizer and two penny buns.

Chapter 20

Double exposure!

During my stay Mrs Slaughter often took us out to see interesting places. Once we went to the miniature village in Beaconsfield. Another time, the circus came to Princes Risborough. We returned home after the show fired with enthusiasm and agreed between us that we would put on our own show. First we tried to ride round the lawn on a bike with someone sitting on the handlebars but dropped the idea when one of the girls got her bottom pinched by the brake lever. I then demonstrated how easy it was to balance a broom on the bridge of the nose until it slipped and nearly poked my eye out. We reluctantly abandoned the whole scheme.

Another outing with the family was to the open-air swimming pool in Aylesbury. My hostess was a very large lady who wore for the occasion a loosely fitting knitted swim-suit. We were all merrily splashing about and jumping up and down in the shallow end when I noticed as she rose above the surface, that due to the weight of water which had entered her cavernous cleavage, the elasticated top of her costume had descended to well beneath her ample bosom.

This was a situation which I was unable to face so I beat a hasty retreat to the other end of the pool to watch developments from the sanctuary of the diving board. Despite screams from a number of teenaged girls, the exposure continued for several minutes until at last one of our young girls raised the alarm whereupon everything was hastily gathered in and tucked away. She immediately left the pool in a glowing and confused state pursued by her children asking: "Do you think anyone saw you, mummy?" I feigned innocence of the entire incident.

Most of the time I was in Whiteleaf I spent alone. I did try the Scouts but it wasn't quite the same as at home. Then I met up with a boy of my own age. We did not set out to cause mayhem but somehow we encouraged the pyromaniac within each of us. Off we went on a jolly jaunt taking with us a box of matches. The hayfield was dry and ready to be harvested so we would be very careful and light only a very small fire. I have never seen flames move so quickly. In no time at all, flames shot across the field towards a hedgerow. We stamped furiously at the flames yelling like lunatics as we did so. We ran hither and thither in blind panic not knowing what to do. The nearest call-box was miles away. We were grey with fear. The whole county could be reduced to ashes. We stopped careering about and stood watching in disbelief at what we had done. We need not have concerned ourselves as the flames, having travelled so fast, rapidly ignited the hay which went up almost like gun-cotton and was unable to sustain enough heat to set fire to the hedge. The flames died down almost as quickly as they had appeared leaving a black swath between where we were standing and the hedge. We sank to the ground with relief, rolled over and lay for several minutes staring at the sky without saying a word. I vowed that I would never, never play with matches again. But of course I did.

There is something about walking through woods which encourages peristalsis in me. I don't know whether it is the smell of leaf-mould or merely the fresh woodland air, but then as now, I risk being caught out in the countryside.

A picnic was organised and off we went. We walked from Whiteleaf up onto the Chiltern hills to a large cross, which had been carved out of the chalk, and trudged on into some woods. As if on cue, disaster struck with such swiftness that by the time I had dodged away from the others to the seclusion of a clump of bushes, it was too late. I did my best to sort myself out with the aid of dock-leaves and after climbing back into my trousers, stuffed my pants into my bag. At all costs the girls were not to learn of my ill-fate, so on returning to the cottage I went straight upstairs to my bedroom to hide the evidence at the bottom of my suitcase.

Some days later while I was in my bedroom reading, the girls burst in and danced excitedly around the room waving an instantly recognisable pair of sparkling white underpants which they had discovered in the week's ironing, their mother having transferred the remainder of my things from my case to a chest of drawers. I tried to deny ownership by suggesting that they were their young brother's. "They're too *big* for him," they giggled. "Well, maybe they're your father's," I suggested unconvincingly. "They're too *small* for him- they're YOURS," they chorused gleefully, "*We* know what happened," they gloated triumphantly. The little devils!

Chapter 21
Eccles

After several months in Buckinghamshire I was told that I was to travel north to stay with the Whitburn family who lived just outside Manchester in a village called Eccles, a name famous for its cakes which might more properly be described as pastries. Mr Whitburn worked for MEL which is where my father got to know him on the occasions when the latest developments in light alloys needed to be patented.

Before leaving for Eccles, my father had, in my view quite unnecessarily, warned me that I should not say things like 'the only good German is a dead one' even though at the time V1s and V2s were raining down on England, because the lady who was to look after me was in fact German. Mrs Whitburn had married before the war so that she had gained dual nationality status and accordingly was not interned. I can recall being completely neutral on the subject of Mrs Whitburn's Germanness. Having been informed that I was to stay with her and that she would feed and look after me, I had judged that she must be a good sort and the fact that our two countries were at war was quite a separate unrelated matter.

Looking back on my time there I now consider the situation a little bizarre especially when regular soirées were held for the purpose of singing Schubertian lieders. A friend would arrive with his 'cello, Mrs Whitburn played the piano and Mr Whitburn sang. If the police had heard the sound of German songs coming from the confines of a blacked-out parlour we could well have been arrested.

Mrs Whitburn was a charming and most tolerant lady and I regarded her as my replacement mother. Frequently she had to resolve, as diplomatically as possible, disputes between her son Frank, two years my junior, and me as I had detected in him some Nazi tendencies. For example, he asserted that the German army were better equipped than the

British army which infuriated me because from my superior knowledge I *knew* that British was always best so he was obviously mistaken. The only way to convince him that he was wrong was to attempt to strangle the blighter. His pleadings quickly brought his mother to the rescue. I am proud to say that I resisted playing the poor evacuee card.

Her tolerance was tested to breaking point when I decided to practise Beethoven's Minuet in G. I must have played that tedious piece of music several hundred times during the course of my stay.

Their daughter was about eighteen and very attractive; so much so that she aroused a passion within me quite blotting out any earlier amorous feelings I might have had towards other young ladies. Despite my tender age of twelve, I was determined make a play for her. There was the minor snag that my voice had not yet broken, so for a whole week I practised speaking in a low voice which I believed would demonstrate a maturity sufficient to impress her. Unfortunately, she was not in the least impressed as the next time we met the first thing she said, in a deliberately low voice to mimic mine, was: "Why are you speaking in that growly voice?" My embarrassment was compounded by the sight of her handsome sailor boyfriend, whose existence was hitherto unknown to me, grinning at me over her shoulder.

Not to be totally upstaged, I asked him why the end of his nose was flat, to which he explained convincingly that he and his shipmates had been practising with their rifles while at sea potting at seagulls and a stray bullet had hit him fair and square right on the end of his nose and he was lucky to be alive to tell the tale. I was ready to accept this perfectly plausible story when she interceded to reassure me that all this was untrue and that his nose had been reshaped due to a fight. It took me a few days to recover my confidence following that little exchange.

I can still perform the arm and hand motion which I learnt when I became a campanologist for two successive weeks. Throughout the first few years of the war bell-ringing was banned except in the case of an invasion. However, by 1944 when the war had distinctly turned in our favour, the joyous sound of church bells was once again heard. I was taken by Mr Whitburn to the Parish Church in Eccles and introduced to all the bell-ringers in the belfry. I had to stand on a box so as to reach the bell-rope of the treble comfortably. The tucked-back end of the rope was gripped by the little and ring fingers of the left hand (I am right-handed) and the red and white tufted tassel (the 'Sally') was gripped by the right hand and the remaining fingers and thumb of the left hand. A gentle pull would set the bell swinging away from its stay whereby the sally would fly upwards at speed. If you didn't let go of the sally you would go up with it. At full stretch the left hand would then bring the rope down adding impetus to the bell, the returning sally giving a little bouncing action before it flew back up again to repeat the cycle.

Incidentally, because the ringing of church bells outside certain hours might be misconstrued as the start of an invasion, the whole chime of bells was 'rung down' after each session. All eight bells ringing in synchronism made a mighty noise. If they had been left up any shock from an explosion might have rocked the bells off their stays and set them off ringing by themselves.

I was never short on cultural activities during my stay in Eccles. In addition to my exposure to Lieder, Beethoven and campanology, I was taken to my first ballet at the Opera House, Manchester. From the archives of the Manchester Central Library I have been able to ascertain that the ballet was Sadlers Wells production of Roussel's 'Le Festin de l'Araignée' (The Spider's Banquet). The butterfly was danced by none other than Moira Shearer (Mrs Ludovic Kennedy) of the famous film 'The Red Shoes' made in 1948. My recall is a little indefinite other than the clear image of a very green stage set which had an elaborate spider's web made of rope from which the ballerina would descend to perform her spidery dance and catch her prey. From that moment on I felt that I had joined the ballet cognoscente. It amazes me to think that a full scale ballet was performed at a time when our country was under bombardment by thousands of flying bombs and rockets. The show had to go on!

Chapter 22

Abersoch

Frank Whitburn had to suffer quite a lot under my dominance, poor fellow. His parents were at pains not to upset me as I was the refugee from the bomb-ravaged South. Apart from the ritual strangleholds he had to endure, he was obliged to concede to occasional selfishness on my part. I had been invited to join the family for a short holiday in North Wales. We stayed in a farm cottage near Abersoch. I can still pronounce the name of the farm but the spelling eludes me. It is something like Tyddn Talgogh Uhogh. In the village store they sold maps and one map in particular, published by Geographia and costing one shilling, caught my attention as it showed the footpaths in the area. Frank also took a fancy to it and an argument ensued as to who would have it. (How could we have had a set-to over a shilling map, there was a war on for goodness' sake.) His mother made a great effort to persuade Frank to drop his claim to ownership of the map which was the only one of its kind in the world and I so badly wanted it. The transaction was completed and the precious map was given to me whereupon, by reason of the fact that Frank had so graciously given in, my purchase became as dross in my hands. I felt very ashamed. A Pyrrhic victory indeed.

Frank gamely came on walks with me. To toughen us up I had decided that for the duration of the week we would go everywhere without shoes. When his feet had become red and sore as we climbed on rocks and stubbed our toes on stones, I agreed that he could wear his plimsolls. So as not to embarrass him, I put mine on. It was a relief not to have to keep up the pretence.

Across the tree-lined main road leading in to Abersoch I noticed that the thick branch of a tree extending across the road met a branch belonging to a tree on the other side of the road. This was too good to miss. We both succeeded in our aerial traverse of the road by shifting along the branches with our legs dangling down on each side, our feet just inches from the tops of lorries that were passing underneath. Excellent sport!

We were allowed to hunt for eggs in the barn as the hens nested there in various nooks. One morning, having returned to the house with the eggs, we went back to climb up onto the bales of hay from where we jumped down onto the loose hay below. Before long many of the bales had been converted into loose hay. The dust got into my chest and as a consequence I was laid low for a day and had to stay in the farmhouse parlour. As I was sitting at the table I glanced towards the door to see the farmer and his wife talking and nodding in my direction. Although they were speaking in Welsh, I had a pretty good idea of what the subject matter of their conversation might be. Welsh turned into English emphatically informing me that their barn was to be out of bounds for the remainder of the holiday.

On the rocks of the promontory which defines the eastern end of Porth Neigwl (Hell's Mouth) we found a herring gull with a broken wing. It offered no resistance when we picked it up to move it to a position where we thought the other birds could perhaps provide food. On our return the next day we found it dead. We dug a hole in the sand into which we reverently laid our poor bird, fixed two bits of driftwood together to make a cross, neatly arranged a few pebbles and watched as the tide came in to envelop the simple grave. Frank and I got along quite well after that.

Chapter 23
Uncle David

My father's brother, Cyril, lived with my aunt Irene and cousin Barbara, in a very large Victorian house in West Dulwich. The occasional visit to their house always signalled adventure and good sport. I would roam through all the rooms from the basement kitchen to the attic. Leading off the green-carpeted entrance hall were a large dining room with a radiogram which could play more than one gramophone record by an ingenious arrangement which dropped the records successively as each record was played, a lounge containing a gleaming grand piano with its lid up and another room which had been adapted as a theatre complete with tip-up seats. A broad staircase swept up from the entrance hall to the first floor in the manner of a Hollywood black and white set. A swing-door gave access to the servants' stairs which were situated at one side of the house and served all of the floors. It was truly a magnificent place for a boy to indulge in all kind of adventures.

It was possible to communicate between the kitchen and some rooms by means of speaking tubes built into the walls. The ends of each tube were provided with a whistle. All you did was to pull out the whistle and blow hard to attract attention by means of the whistle at the other end. My testing of the facility merely met with abuse.

The house had a 'dumb-waiter' which I found entertaining. It was intended for conveying the meals from the kitchen to the ground floor dining room. I had other ideas. For me, it was a miniature lift. I could just about squeeze into the cage and managed to haul myself up and down the lift-shaft. Having found myself midway between floors and unable to move it was necessary to call plaintively for help. More abuse.

In the entrance hall there was a gong of seemingly Rank-size proportions, which hung on a wooden stand. To summon everyone to

Sunday lunch I was permitted to bang the gong using a stick with a chamois leather ball on the end. Every time I worked up a really good volume of sound, someone stepped forward to spoil my fun.

The view from the rear windows of the house, especially from the attic windows, was dominated by the north tower of the remains of the Crystal Palace which burnt down in 1936. I didn't actually see the flames but I do remember being shown from the front door of our house the red glow in the sky as the fire raged. The tower was later demolished because, as it was explained to me, 'it might serve as a landmark for the German bombers.' My parents' description of the fire could almost match that of Du Maurier's 'Manderley.' They evoked vivid images of crashing metal structures and the molten glass which ran in torrents down Anerley Hill. Many people found it difficult to understand how such an edifice, constructed primarily of steel and glass, could be totally destroyed by fire. My father's memory of the Crystal Palace was when he played the violin in a one thousand strong youth orchestra conducted by Sir Henry Wood who founded the Promenade Concerts.

During the late thirties I was told that Uncle Cyril was now, for the purpose of better marketing himself for the Silver Screen, to be known as David Farrar.

He appeared in many films during the war and on into the fifties and sixties. Of his wartime films I saw 'Went The Day Well?' which starred Leslie Banks, Thora Hird, Glynis Johns, her father Mervyn Johns, to name but a few. It is a story of a village being captured by a group of German parachutists who were ultimately defeated by the courage of all the villagers as they overcame adversity despite the sinister collaboration of one quisling. In the gun battle at the denouement, as our Thora picked off the enemy as she did ducks in the shooting gallery at Blackpool, one of the heroes was hit by rifle fire. In response to an enquiry as to his health he was heard to reply: "Only shooting pains!"

My uncle played Leutnant Jung who shot the vicar as he rang the

Uncle David starred with Deborah Kerr in
'Black Narcissus' (1946)

church bell to summon help. A few years ago I visited the village of Turville in Buckinghamshire which was the location for the film, also used incidentally, for the BBC TV series 'The Vicar of Dibley.' I looked around the beautiful church and met some ladies arranging flowers. On hearing the tale of my Uncle's dastardly deed one of them remarked: "I wish you would shoot our vicar!" from which I gathered that she was not too taken with the then present incumbent. I also met a 90-year-old gentleman who remembered seeing all the actors and film crew back in 1942. The film is a wonderful piece of propaganda and has been used by the Open University in their popular culture study course for teaching 'deconstruction'.

There was a young actor who should have had a mention in the credits of 'Went The Day Well?' and that was Gerald Moore (not the pianist), a fellow former pupil of Eltham College, whom I met only recently. He was the boy in the film who, whilst attempting to take an SOS message written on an egg to the next village, was knocked off his bicycle into a duck-pond by a passing car, thus keeping us all on tenter-hooks for another reel. Gerald's career as an actor faltered due largely to his being vertically challenged so instead he followed a highly successful path from acting to dentistry and then on to surgery, writing and surreal art.

Chapter 24

Auntie May

A few weeks before the end of the war someone called unexpectedly. My mother went to answer the bell and with the door ajar held a brief conversation with the caller who was asked to wait a few moments on the doorstep while I was sent upstairs to occupy myself in my attic workshop. What was the mystery? Why was my mother behaving so conspiratorially? Why all the whispering? Curiosity having got the better of me, I watched from my bedroom at the front of the house whereupon an hour later I saw the departing figure of a lady I had not seen for three years. It was my lovely Auntie May, my mother's younger sister, no longer dressed in her smart WAAF's uniform.

I ran downstairs to ask why my aunt did not want to see me. In the present liberal times one would accept an unintended pregnancy, sorry, er- happy event, as a matter of course. However, it so happened that this particular happy event was anything but happy. My mother explained to me that my aunt had been stationed at an RAF base near Manchester where she had made friends with an airman. My poor aunt had sobbed her story to my mother, explaining that she would have to bring up the baby alone because the man would not leave his wife. To this explanation of the evidently appalling scandal I made no comment as at the time I had no thoughts on the matter. On reflection, it seems a pity that my distressed aunt should have been treated like a leper. Sadly, that was the last I ever saw of my aunt and I didn't even have the opportunity to say goodbye. I may have a cousin somewhere, maybe more, unknown to me.

A few months after my aunt's visit we had another caller who arrived unannounced. Once again I was dispatched to the far end of the house as my mother ushered in an old man who, after the ritual cup of tea, left. It turned out that my dismissal was again for the avoidance of my mother's shame. The gentleman in question was my mother's father, in other words my grandfather, whom I had never seen. I had heard stories about him, how he came home drunk on paydays and threw what was left of his pay-packet on the kitchen floor for all nine children to scramble to pick up the money and give it to their mother. This sad widower, who had called to pay his respects after many years absent from the family, was kept at arm's length. It seemed strange to me that I could not see my own grandfather. Clearly my mother, who was generally a very sympathetic person, having shaken herself free from a poor working class background to enjoy the comforts of middle-class Sidcup, had no wish to involve herself once again with her origins. Her resentment remained. To her, her father was an undesirable who was not to taint her children by his presence. Hence, there were to be no cheery introductions. The chapter was positively closed.

Chapter 25

Victory

After a war lasting five years and nine months, the German armed forces surrendered unconditionally on the 7th May 1945 and hostilities ceased. Victory in Europe was declared on the 8th May and the official celebrations began within a few weeks. We stood at the roadside to watch the Victory Parade marching through Sidcup. We clapped and cheered as each of the organisations represented passed by. I remember particularly our own regiment, the Royal West Kents and the Home Guard (Dad's Army). Most impressive to me was the Air Training Corps contingent whose colour sergeant, in smart white gauntlets, showed off to my complete satisfaction. Every fifty yards or so he would launch his silver mace high into the air and then, unfailingly, catch it one-handed with a resounding thwack on leather.

Within a few weeks following the surrender the Gaumont and Pathe News pictures of the liberation of the concentration camps were shown in the cinemas. We sat stupefied and silent on seeing the awful cruelty that had taken place; silent, that is, until a sorry-looking dog was seen trotting among the ruins and human degradation at which point the audience let out an incongruous "ah" to relieve the tension.

The Pacific Campaign raged on for another few months with enormous losses on both sides. The Americans took three months to take the island of Okinawa. Japanese Kamikaze pilots flew their bomb-laden aircraft into the allied warships in a vain attempt to stave off the inevitable demise of the Japanese empire. Finally, after an atomic bomb called 'Little Boy' was dropped on Nagasaki on August 6th, followed by another called 'Fat Man' over Hiroshima, the Japanese high command capitulated on August 10th.

The total number of deaths from these two bombs will never be known because of people dying later from the effects of radiation. A figure of 240,000 has been mooted. At thirteen I was old enough to appreciate that war was unpleasant. It was difficult to feel an overwhelming degree of sympathy when hearing about all those Japanese men, women and children dying because the Japanese soldiers had inflicted such terrible acts of cruelty upon our prisoners of war. They had also carried out the never-to-be-forgotten attack on Pearl Harbor on that fateful day in December 1941.Therefore I, like most other people, was only too pleased that Victory over Japan had finally been achieved, despite the civilian death toll, and that many lives would be saved as a result.

It is estimated that the World War II caused, in one way or another, the deaths of in excess of fifty million human beings (50,000,000) which is like saying five hundred times the number of spectators in the Millennium Stadium when full. Of course, I was unaware of the scale of the slaughter. I was told at the time about our merchant seaman drowning in oily seas after U-Boats had torpedoed many of our ships bringing much needed supplies to our shores. I needed little encouragement from my mother to urge me to eat up the food which had arrived on my plate with such sacrifice. It was a shock to read the newspaper headlines announcing the disintegration of the battle-cruiser HMS Hood which my father said was possibly hit in the magazine by a shell from the German ~~pocket~~ battleship Bismarck with the loss of 1,418 sailors (three were rescued). Better were the headlines a few days later trumpeting the sinking of the Bismarck, with its crew of over 2,200 (110 were rescued).

I joined in the feeling of relief felt that the tide of war was at last beginning to turn in our favour when we heard in August 1942 of the first great British victory at El Alemein (North Africa) led by General Montgomery. Names like Benghazi, Tobruk and Tripoli became common words in my ten-year-old vocabulary. In the same month our spirits sank on receiving the sad news of the disastrous raid on Dieppe in which so many lives were lost, mostly Canadian. The successful Dambusters raid in which three German dams were breached using Barnes Wallis' 'bouncing bomb' gave us something to lift our spirits though many aircrews were lost. Reference to the D-Day landings in Normandy and the Arnhem débâcle should not be omitted nor passed over lightly but I shall have to stop here and refer you to the many historians who have brilliantly analysed and explained the amazing campaigns and acts of heroism which took place throughout WWII. In the appendix to my memoirs I have listed a few of the books of those in my possession which have been of particular interest to me.

The above described memories and many more are lodged irrevocably in my mind. As extraordinary and memorable as these events are, I have to admit that they were somewhat remote from me in terms of involvement. They were happening elsewhere and therefore didn't concern me greatly. I plead in self-defence that, even though aware of the significant dramatic actions taking place, I was too young to take in fully the enormity of what was going on in the world.

To have survived the Blitz, the flying bombs and the rockets, I attribute to a large helping of good fortune and to the protection given to me by my parents who lovingly cared for me as they always did and to the many others who risked and often gave their lives.

Now it was all over. I was a little sorry that nothing was happening to replace the experience of 'living.' No more Spitfires and Hurricanes making vapour trails. No more friendly barrage balloons. No heart-stopping wail of the siren. No more bangs either by me or the enemy. All was very quiet. Nevertheless, I was grateful that the killing had ceased.

On the day when Victory in Europe was declared, our neighbours gathered in the front gardens to congratulate each other on their survival and to reflect on their experiences. The relief was palpable. They had suffered two world wars in thirty-one years. For my part, I wished to express my joy with my own youthful high spirits. So, grabbing my Union Jack, I climbed onto the potting shed roof and from there onto the sloping roof of our house. I ran up to the pitched roof and edged my way along the ridge tiles to the gable end at the front of the house and sat with my legs dangling over the roof verge. From my lofty perch thirty feet up and in a fit of exhibitionism to impress my parents and neighbours gathered on the lawn below, I waved the flag furiously and shouted "Hooray" several times at the top of my voice. I didn't receive the reaction I was looking for. The smiles on their faces instantly evaporated. To my utter dismay, my mother shouted frantically: "Come down. You'll fall!"

Parents simply don't understand us.

Bibliography

Winston.S.Churchill, *The Second World War*

Philip Ziegler, *London At War*

Lewis Blake, *Red Alert*

Edgar Holt, *The World At War*

Len Deighton, *Fighter*

John Sweetman, *The Dambusters Raid*

Nick Yapp, *The Hulton Getty Picture Collection 1940s*

Richard Hough & Denis Richards, *The Battle of Britain*

Bob Ogley, *Doodlebugs and Rockets*

Arthur Bryant, *The Alanbrooke War Diaries*

Elizabeth-Anne Wheal & Stephen Pope, *The Dictionary of the Second World War*

Raynes Minns, *Bombers & Mash*

Anne Harvey, *In Time Of War (Selection of War Poetry)*

John Mercer, *Sidcup*

Penelope Houston, *"Went The Day Well?"*

Hugh Smallwood, *2nd TAF SPITFIRE*

INDEX

A

Abersoch   95
Altmark   46
Alvar Liddell   58
Anderson   52,57
Athenia   46
Aylesbury   85,86,87

B

Barnes Wallis   105
Battle of Britain   49,50
BBC Home Service   18
Beaconsfield   87
Belgium   46
Bell Ringing   92,93
Betts, Phyllis (Miss)   39
Bews, Denis   5,70
Biggs, Frank   57
Biggs, May   101
Birkbeck Road   21
Bismarck, ~~Pocket~~ Battleship   104
Black Horse   17
Blackfen   51
Blake, Quentin   43
Blitz   51,81,82,105
Blue Rose   17
Bolton (Mrs)   42,43
Boscombe   29
Brandenburg Gate   26
British Restaurant   21
Broadstairs   30
Brown, Joan (Miss)   67
Bryant, Rob   5
Buckinghamshire   85,91,100

Burnt Oak Lane	11,13,14,26,35
Butcher Curnow	18

C

Campanology	92,93
Cannock House	41
Captain Oates	14
Carter Paterson	16
Catford	73
Chappell's	18
Chariots of Fire	65
Chartered Institute of Patent Agents	25
Chislehurst	63,78
Christchurch Road	59
Collins, Patricia	5
Congregational Church	21
Cornwall	11,47
Crabb, Doug	67
Crocken Hill	75
Crystal Palace	98
Cubs	21,63

D

Daily Herald	18
Daily Telegraph	13,45
Dambusters	104
D-Day	77,104
de Warrenne, Jill	5
Defiant	47
Dieppe	104
Doodle-bugs	18,53,77,78,79,81,91,105
Dorniers	57
Dunkirk	47

E

Ealing Studios	16

Eccles	91,93
El Alemein	104
Eltham	41,49
Eltham College	22,65,67,68,71,74,75
Eric Thomas	18

F

Farrar, Barbara	97
Farrar, David	97,99,100
Farrar, Irene	97
Fenton, Molly	5
Flying Bombs	18,53,77,78,79,81,91,105
Flying Fortress	86
Focke-Wulf 190	73,75
Foxwell's	16
France	46

G

Gas-masks	65,81
George Higgins	18
Germany	25,26,27,46
Goddard's	18
Gormenghast	72
Grace, Carolyn	5,48
Grace, Nick	47
Graf Spee	46
Grafton (Mrs)	39
Grassington Road	63
Great War	45,61

H

Heinkels	57
Hell's Mouth	96
Henry Wood, Sir	98
High Street, Sidcup	17
Hiroshima	103

Hither Green 73
Hitler, Adolf 19,25,59,78
HMS Cossack 46
HMS Hood 104
Holy Trinity Church 18
Home & Colonial 16
Hope and Glory 51
Hurricane 47,105

I

Ian Allen 83
Italy 77
ITMA 19

J

Jones, Dora (Miss) 73,75

K

King's Row 16

L

Lamorbey C of E Primary School 18,41,42,43
Lamorbey Park Hotel 14
Lane's 17
Le Festin d'Araignée 5
Liddell, Eric 65
Light Rescue 53,82
London 33,49,51,81
Lord Woolton 60
Luftwaffe 49,57

M

Mackay, Carol 5,33,81
Macky 71,72,85
Maginot Line 45
Magnesium Elektron Limited 25,91

Manchester	5,91,93,101
Manchester Library	5,93
Manor House	33
Marlborough Park Avenue	12,14,35,52,78
Martin's Bank	16
Matthews, Alice	11,101
Matthews, Bee	5
Matthews, Daphne	5
Matthews, Mary	11,12,29
Matthews, Nicholas	5,81
Matthews, Stanley	13,25,26,52
Maypole	16
McIver, Matthew (Mr)	71,72,85
Medway Queen	47
Messerschmitts	57
Milnes, Alan	5
Moira Shearer	93
Montgomery, General	104
Moore, Gerald	100
Mosquito	50
Moss Bros	28
Mulberry Harbour	77

N

Nagasaki	103
National Archives	5
Naylor, John	5
New Eltham	33
Normandy	77,105

O

Odeon Cinema	18
Open University	100
Operation Barbarossa	50
Operation Sealion	49
Oxfordshire	85

P

Pacific Campaign	103
Park House	41
Patent Attorneys	25
Patent Office	25
Peake, Mervyn	72
Pearl Harbor	104
Peckham	11,12
Phoney War	46,47
Porth Neigl	96
Potter's	17
Powles, David	5
Princes Risborough	87

Q

Queens Mary's Hospital	53

R

RAF	49,82,101
Red Shoes	93
Regal Cinema	16
River Plate	46
River Thames	49
Roadknight's	19
Rockets	77,78,81,91,105

S

San Demitrio London	16
Sandhurst Road	73,75
Saward, Michael	67
Schubert, Erich	28
Scouts	21,87
September 3rd 1939	45
Sharpington, Vernon	78
Shrapnel	51
Sidcup	11,12,15,16,21,22,41,43,65,78,79,103

Siegfried Line   45,46
Skinner, Ron   63
Slaughter Family   33,82,84,87
Smith, Peter M.   5
Smoky Joe   65
Snow White and the Seven Dwarfs   17
South London Iron Company   18,57
Southam, Brian   5
Spicer's   18
Spider's Banquet   93
Spitfire   5,47,48,105
Stanley Dunn   18
Stirlings   57

T
Thompson, Doug   67
Tommy Handley   19
Turville   100

U
U-Boats   46,103
USAAF   86

V
V1s   18,53,77,78,79,91
V2s   77,78,81,91,105
VE-Day   103,105
VJ-Day   103
von Braun   78

W
Walthamstow Hall   67
Wellingtons   57
Went The Day Well?   98
Whitburn Family   91,95
White, Gregory   5

Whiteleaf	82,84,87,88
Whitleys	57
Willes, John	14,67
Winston Churchill	50
Worsley	81
Wyatt, Arthur	71